Lady Anne Clifford

1590–1676

GORDON THORBURN

FONTHILL

Fonthill Media Language Policy

Fonthill Media publishes in the international English language market. One language edition is published worldwide. As there are minor differences in spelling and presentation, especially with regard to American English and British English, a policy is necessary to define which form of English to use. The Fonthill Policy is to use the form of English native to the author. Gordon Thorburn was born and educated in the UK; therefore British English has been adopted in this publication.

Fonthill Media Limited
Fonthill Media LLC
www.fonthillmedia.com
office@fonthillmedia.com

First published in the United Kingdom and the United States of America 2020

British Library Cataloguing in Publication Data:
A catalogue record for this book is available from the British Library

ISBN 978-1-78155-771-6

Typeset in 10.5pt on 13pt Sabon
Printed and bound in England

CONTENTS

Author's Note

In our modern society, it is easy to forget just how important the Christian religion was in England in the period we are covering here, the sixteenth and seventeenth centuries. It was not a question of whether you believed, it was intrinsic to daily life, it was taken as read, it was a fact. Going to church was compulsory, by the Act of Uniformity, 1569:

> And that from and after the said Feast of the Nativity of Saint John Baptist next coming, all and every Person and Persons inhabiting within this Realm, or any other the Queen's Majesty's Dominions, shall diligently and faithfully, having no lawful or reasonable excuse to be absent, endeavour themselves, to resort to their Parish Church or Chapel accustomed … upon every Sunday, and other days ordained or used to be kept as Holy-days.

The penalties for not going were public censure by the Church and a fine of 12 pence, which for an ordinary working person would have been as painful as £150 today, relieved only by the thought that it was going to 'the use of the Poor of the same Parish'.

The subject of our story, Lady Anne Clifford, was perhaps more religious than some of her social equals, especially the men, but she was not exceptional in that. We can also be sure that she was a true believer and not one who thought to buy her way to heaven with endowments and gifts.

The purpose of the biblical quotations in the story, therefore, is not to persuade readers into the ways of Lady Anne but simply to put her story into her own daily context. In her diaries and other writings, she frequently cites verses from the Bible, generally just noting chapter and verse numbers rather than quoting in full, the assumption being that the Bible was well known enough not to need quoting, and she rarely forgets to mention the Christian round alongside the everyday, the commonplace, and the historically weighty.

> Upon the 28th [December 1616] I dined above in my Chamber & wore my Night Gown because I was not very well, which day and yesterday I forgot it was Fish day and ate Flesh at both Dinners. In the afternoon I played at Glecko with my Lady Gray and lost £27 and odd money.
>
> The King asked us all [20 January 1617] if we would submit to his Judgement in this Case. My Uncle Cumberland, my Coz. Clifford & my Lord [husband, earl of Dorset] answered they would, but I would never agree to it without Westmoreland, at which the King grew in a great Chaffe, my Lord of Pembroke and the King's Solicitor speaking much against me.
>
> Upon the 5th [March 1617], Couch puppied in the morning. The 8th I made an end of reading Exodus with Mr Ran [Knole chaplain]. After Supper I played at Glecko with the Steward as I often do after Dinner and Supper.

Glecko was a card game, probably a simple one of luck and betting, and not the well-known game called gleek, which was complex and for three players.

We must also apologise for the poor variety of Christian names in those days, and hope that readers will be able to steer their way through the plethora of Margarets and Roberts.

> 1 Esdras III x: The first wrote, Wine is the strongest. The second wrote, the King is the strongest. The third wrote, Women are the strongest: But above all things Truth beareth away the victory.

1

Mother and Father

Lady Anne's mother, Margaret Russell, was born in 1560; Margaret's mother, also Margaret, Countess of Bedford, one of the St Johns of Bletsoe, died two years later of smallpox, so the little girl was sent to live with an aunt, Alice, Lady Elmes, at Lilford Hall in Northamptonshire. This Tudor mansion, built in 1495 by 'a merchant of very wonderfulle richnesse', and its extensive parkland so engendered in young Margaret the love of the peaceful, rural life that, over thirty years later, she would send her own daughter there, 'which caused this Mother and Daughter ever after to love a Country life the better, they being both there Seasoned with the ground of goodness and religion' (from Lady Anne's diary).

Margaret was the youngest of seven; the eldest was Anne, who married the earl of Warwick, Ambrose Dudley, in 1565 at the age of sixteen, when already a maid of honour to Queen Elizabeth. This aunt to Lady Anne, the countess of Warwick, was 'a great friend to virtue' and would always be held in the deepest affection by her niece as well as by the queen.

Margaret went back to the family seat, Chenies Manor, on the Buckinghamshire–Hertfordshire border, aged about nine, where a sister and two of her brothers were still living, along with a husband-to-be. The law of magnetism states that unlike poles attract, which seems to have been borne out by the teenagers Margaret Russell and George Clifford, who were described by Lady Anne: 'She was pensive and delicate, he adventurous and fond of display'. Margaret was also said to be handsome, graceful, well read, courteous to all, and strong willed, with a sharp mind of scientific bent. This is not to say that George was not likewise handsome, graceful, educated, *et cetera*, but he did like a bet and he was a tearaway.

Said Lady Anne of her mother: 'Her spirit never yielded to ill fortune or opposition', which characteristics would be much needed in one married to a young man whose own personality led him simultaneously into national hero status and crippling debt.

Lady Anne's father, George Clifford, was born in 1558 at Brougham castle in Westmoreland. Grandfather Henry, 2nd earl of Cumberland and 12th baron de Clifford, died when George was eleven, in 1569, making him 13th baron and 3rd earl but a minor and so in need of a ward. His mother was alive, but she was not granted the wardship. Queen Elizabeth gave that to Francis Russell, 2nd earl of Bedford, who requested it because there was already an arrangement made between Bedford and George's late father that there would be a marriage of the Cliffords and the Russells.

Bedford had been imprisoned by Queen Mary for his reformist religious views and for being part of the Lady Jane Grey conspiracy, but he literally battled his way back into favour by leading an English army fighting in France for Philip II of Spain, then scheduled to be Queen Mary's husband. It would seem that Lady Anne's sterling qualities did not come only through the Clifford genes.

Bedford became a great man of state under Queen Elizabeth while his future son-in-law, George, lived with his future bride and the other Russell playmates at Chenies Manor, and he would have been there when the queen visited for four weeks in 1570. The marriage happened in 1577 with Queen Elizabeth a guest, when Margaret was aged seventeen, and it all began as an affectionate and happy alliance, as is clear from George's letters to his young bride, addressed to 'My sweet Meg' and 'My Deare Love', and signed 'Thyne till death, whatsoever happens' and 'Yours from all others'. One signature, 'Wishing to God that you may doe in all this, and in all other things, what is pleasantest for you' might have been more accurately written to himself.

The earl and new countess of Cumberland made their first home at Skipton castle, where George's mother, the Dowager Countess Anne, was living. The young couple lived fairly quietly, with occasional trips to their or their relatives' halls and castles, but Margaret fell ill. Visits to Buxton in Derbyshire were prescribed to take the waters, and with or without their benefit, she recovered sufficiently to give birth. The first child, Francis, was born in 1584; the second, Robert, in 1585, soon after Margaret's father died. Her brother, Francis, died on the same day, killed in a skirmish on the Scottish borders. Lady Anne wrote of this period of the marriage:

> And after this tedious tyme of sickness was past it pleased God to bless this virtuous lady with the extreme love and affection of her husband, which lasted about nyne or tenne years towards her, but little more.

Much of the extreme love was expressed at a distance by now, the earl having begun his lifelong dedication to gambling and self-promotion at court. Before his marriage, George had been a scholar of mathematics at Trinity College, Cambridge, and of geography at Oxford—entry to the universities in those days did not require proof of ability; money and titles were qualifications enough—which led him into the relatively new science of navigation and, later, into the older business of piracy, or privateering, which is an unreliable trade.

Equally unreliable were his chief enjoyments, being horse racing, bear baiting, bowling matches, and any other game he could wager on. Still, the estates were large, with castles and farms by the score, and they could absorb a certain degree of prodigality but could not provide the kind of income necessary for a great man at court with an image to keep up. The remedy of the day lay overseas, Spanish gold and other riches to be discovered in the New World, and George would eventually fund no fewer than eleven expeditions to faraway lands, some of which made a profit.

Other buccaneers became more famous in history, such as Drake, Hawkins, and Ralegh, but at the time, George Clifford was a national hero and a queen's favourite. Her Majesty dropped a glove one day, supposedly on purpose, and was so gratified by Clifford's returning it to her on bended knee, vowing to serve her all his days, that she gave it to him as a favour. In 1587, he was a witness at the execution of Mary, Queen of Scots, and the following year, he was again with Drake and Hawkins in the prosecution of the queen's enemies.

On 20 July 1588, an officer of the queen's navy, Captain Fleming, who had been cruising a frigate of the line in the English Channel, brought word into Plymouth of a mighty fleet of a size without precedent, which he had spied the day before. The wind that was taking this fleet up the Channel was a contrary wind to that in Plymouth harbour, and the tide there too was flowing in. While the fleet sailed past, when it could have sunk the English in their haven, Vice-Admiral Drake was playing bowls on Plymouth Hoe.

'The enemy fleet is here!' they cried, but Sir Francis knew that the wind and tide prevented him getting out to do anything about it, so he might as well finish his game, which he said he had time for and to beat the enemy too.

With the ebb tide, late into the night and early next morning, Her Majesty's fleet was assembled at sea, being about eighty sail, in four squadrons commanded by Admiral Lord Howard of Effingham, Vice-Admiral Drake, Rear-Admiral Sir John Hawkins, and Sir Martin Frobisher. Lord Effingham was not the greatest seaman, but he was able, by his good judgement, to bring together such a group of pirates, cut throats, and chancers into a united fighting force for queen and country, when otherwise they might have been more concerned with claiming prizes for themselves.

By about 1 p.m., the English came in sight of the enemy, which was something of 150 ships of every kind, sailing in a half-moon form. One point of the moon was said to be two leagues to the west of the Eddystone Rock and the other several miles beyond. Their galleons were like castles on the sea, unlike anything ever seen on home waters. While the enemy proceeded in stately fashion towards the Low Countries, where an army awaited embarkation for invasion, the smaller English fleet got both to leeward and windward, whence they cautiously spied upon their quarry. It was seen that many of those ships were not warships at all, but carrying troops. Their tactic would be to come alongside and take their victory by boarding. The English tactic was to stay at a distance and fire cannon into their crowded ranks.

Lord Effingham had no declaration of war to give him leave, so he had need of a gauntlet to throw down, and this he decided was in the shape of one of the smaller and more nimble of the ships in his squadron, called the *Distain*. A message was sent by pinnace, with an order to her commander to attack, fire, and run, as at the tilt, which he did. There was no sign of the Spanish turning round, so war could be declared. One story has the commander of the *Distain* as none other than the earl of Cumberland, a man who gave no way to any pirate or buccaneer on this Earth, but he was almost certainly aboard a bigger ship, the fifty-gun *Elizabeth Bonaventure* that previously carried Drake into Cadiz harbour to singe the king of Spain's beard. The naval officer in charge of the *Bonaventure* was Captain George Raymond, but George Clifford was in command, recently returned from his first treasure-seeking sally abroad to the coast of South America.

There are no records of individual victories in the *Bonaventure*, but the earl is said to have carried the news of the over-all triumph to the queen at Tilbury, where, later, she would deliver her speech with the famous lines 'I have the body of a weak, feeble woman; but I have the heart and stomach of a king, and of a king of England too'.

The next year, while another voyage crossed the oceans commissioned by the earl, the Clifford heir Francis died, aged five, with his mother carrying a baby due in two months. Brother Robert was sickly and George was hoping very much for another boy, but in January 1590, a girl was born at Skipton castle, to be christened Anne. If George was disappointed, he hid it well. Here is part of a letter he wrote a month later (spelling modernised):

> My sweet Meg,
> The happy news of thy safe delivery more gladded me than anything I heard or saw since I saw thee and sweet Meg, as it hath pleased God thus to please thee with the long desired wish (which is more welcome to me than anything else in the world could have been) so with merry heart and thoughts comfort thyself, as thou mayest the sooner recover thy former strength to His praise and my chiefest comfort. I stayed this bearer some days, in hope myself should have delivered this, but the not coming of my ship, which is yet stayed by contrary winds, will not suffer me.

The second heir, Robert, died like his brother, aged five years and eight months, in 1591, with George at sea again heading for the West Indies. The little Lady Anne, at one year and four months old, was now sole heir to both parents and, by right, would be Baroness Clifford, Westmoreland, and Vescy, high sheriffess of that county and lady of the Honour of Skipton-in-Craven.

George's disappointment was mellowed somewhat later in the year when he was appointed Queen Elizabeth's champion, as Sir Henry Lee retired after twenty years in the post. Sir Henry, long a favourite of the queen, held lands in Oxfordshire, including, it was said, the well and bower, now in ruins, of the trysting house built by Henry II for Lady Anne's ancestor, Rosamund the Fair. George Clifford seems to have anticipated his new post by ordering, a couple of years earlier, one of the most spectacular suits of armour ever made in England.

At a modern cost equivalent of about £1 million, he had the decoration in gold of the Tudor rose, the *fleur-de-lis*, and the symbol of Elizabeth, two E's back to back. It was made in Henry VIII's royal workshops at Greenwich, for jousting rather than real battle, of course, and it represents the pinnacle of the Elizabethan/Jacobean armourer's art (now to be seen at the Metropolitan Museum of Art in New York). The earl was further raised in the world when the queen appointed him one of the twenty-four Companions of the Most Noble Order of the Garter in 1592.

To be champion meant that Cumberland rode, as it were, instead of the queen in the lists. In Nicholas Hilliard's painting of him in his champion's jousting outfit, the famous glove can clearly be seen. He liked to play the Knight of Pendragon, after Pendragon castle at Mallerstang, part of the Clifford estates in Westmoreland. This place was associated in legend with King Uther Pendragon, father of King Arthur, although a rather more factual previous owner was Sir Hugh de Morville, one of the four knights who murdered St Thomas Becket in 1170.

George Clifford lived up to the reputation of the dragon-conquering saint he was named after, and his dragonish tilts were much to the queen's liking, though not every opponent would topple the queen's man, which, in effect, would be toppling Her Majesty. He went about everything in life with the same dash. While his loving wife was of a prudent and steady nature, George was a risk taker, and the bigger the risk, the better he liked it. By the time Anne was born and the earl was champion, this aspect of his reputation was well established.

Poor fortune attended the earl's subsequent nautical adventures, although he had the backing of the queen, who loaned him ships from the royal fleet and wrote him flattering letters, addressed to her 'Right trusty and well-beloved Cousin'. While Drake could sack a town in the West Indies and come home with 300,000 ducats (gold and silver coins) and other immeasurable wealth, whenever Clifford made a coup, such as the capture of a Spanish galleon, storms, questions at law or other forces always conspired to deny him his reward. He drained his fortune even further by having his own ship built, the thirty-eight-gun *Scourge of Malice*, but nothing of value ever came of that and he sold it to the newly formed East India Company in 1601 for £3,700 (roughly £7.5 million today) who renamed it *Red Dragon*. That seems to have curbed the earl's excesses for a while.

I Kings X xxii: Once in three years came the navy of Tharshish, bringing gold, and silver, ivory, and apes, and peacocks.

2

To be a Clifford

They came from Norman warlords, the Cliffords. The way the Cliffords liked to tell it, Lady Anne's forebears sailed with the Conqueror to become earls and champions and heirs to the throne. That they became earls and the like cannot be disputed, and there is some truth in 'sailed with the Conqueror', although there was no-one on the ships called Clifford.

In 1067 or soon after, the first Norman earl of Hereford, one William Fitz Osbern, definitely a conquering sailor and fighter at Hastings, took a fancy to a site on the River Wye for a castle, from which he could impose the Norman will upon the Saxon riffraff of west Herefordshire and defend the king's realm against the unruly and itching Welsh. The site was on a hill above a ford, with something of a cliff falling below, and this is usually given as the reason for the name, although it is also possible that there was a fork in the river at the time, a cleft or clift ford. In any case, Clifford castle, near Hay, in the Welsh Marches, was built and gradually made mighty, with a settlement around it. Thus the name was coined but awaited a family to take it.

The next Fitz Osbern, Roger, quarrelled with the Conqueror and lost the argument. His fall from favour gave the castle to his mother's family, called de Toeni, whose male representatives were also at the Battle of Hastings. When they sided wrongly in the wars between King Stephen and Queen Matilda, the then-steward of the estate, Walter Fitz Richard Fitz Pons, decided to shorten himself to Walter de Clifford and, as a steward sometimes will when the master is away, took to himself the role of master.

One of the de Toeni girls, Margaret, granddaughter of the Hastings knight, was a great beauty—a great beauty, indeed. Walter was a powerful and persuasive character, and a consequence of his persuasion was a baby girl. As Walter and Margaret de Clifford set about living the life of country lords, they watched this daughter, Jane, grow into a young woman whose loveliness surpassed all, even her mother's, even 'the face that launched a thousand ships and burnt the topless towers of Ilium', as Marlowe has it. Walter and Margaret would have agreed that, had their daughter made a fourth contestant at the judgement of Paris, all the bribes of Hera, Athena, and Aphrodite would have been insufficient to sway the verdict away from Jane.

There was an occasion when the new king, Henry II, was down their way and Jane was put in his path. King Henry was smitten. Jane listened to the king, and smiled, and gazed, was dainty in her allurement, but did not allow so much as a kiss. Her mother had told her to hold hard for a while. Soon, the king was sighing and protesting his love above all else and composing long poems in which he renamed her the 'Rose of the World', the fairest of the fair, his heart's only desire on earth. Jane, or '*Rosa Mundi*' as she now was, might have wondered what the king's wife would make of all this. That wife, Eleanor of Aquitaine, possibly the wealthiest and most powerful woman of her day, had led troops into battle on the Crusades. Did the king not think she might be put out of temper if she knew he was writing poetry, and not to her?

Apparently not, because, according to legend, Rosamund de Clifford was installed in a secret trysting spot in the forest near Woodstock, which was a villa or small palace of the utmost luxuriousness, with servants and guardians by the dozen, and her every smallest wish granted on the instant. There, she is said to have borne the king two sons, one who became an earl and the other an archbishop. It might be noted that two of Henry's other sons, King Richard the Lionheart and King John of the Magna Carta, rose higher, but they were Queen Eleanor's and had the start on everyone else.

Alas for Rosamund, her trysting spot was so well hidden beyond a labyrinth of secret paths that only those who knew about the guiding silver thread could find their way in. Queen Eleanor discovered the secret, went in, and there poisoned her rival to death. Or some say Rosamund died at the age of forty-five in Clifford castle, in 1176, without the queen's assistance, or at Godstow Abbey, Oxford, where she had previously been educated by the nuns, also in 1176 but at the age of thirty. That Jane de Clifford was King Henry II's mistress for a considerable time is a fact, and this relationship consolidated her father's flimsy claim to the castle and estate.

The de Cliffords marched on through the years, acquiring power, lands, and pride, resisting all attempts by the male line of de Toenis to claim their castle back. Llewellyn, Prince of Wales, married the daughter of King John, and their daughter married a de Clifford, another Walter. This Walter's son, Roger, married into the de Viteripont (Vieuxpont) family, and with his bride, Isabella, came considerable estates in Westmoreland and Cumberland, including Brougham castle, which being beside Penrith was a bulwark against the Scots, and there were de Viteripont castles too at Appleby, Brough, and Mallerstang. These would all become central to the life of Lady Anne, although at the time, there was little to commend them or the immediate area.

Much of the fertile part of Westmoreland, from Cross Fell (Fiend's Fell at it was) to Keswick and beyond to the Solway Firth, was taken up with Inglewood Forest, the largest royal hunting ground in England, where no one was allowed to live, fell a tree, take a dog, or, of course, hunt a deer. The peasantry in the rest of Westmoreland scratched a living somehow, but there was very little in the way of rents and taxes to make the Norman landlords rich.

The majority of the Cliffords' wealth came from their estates in Hereford and the Welsh border regions, and with wealth and position came obligations to the crown. While fulfilling fame, fighting against the Welsh, Roger died by drowning, and his successor, eldest son Robert of Appleby, had his fights at the other end of the country against the Scots. He was with King Edward Longshanks defeating William Wallace at the Battle of Falkirk, 1298, and in 1299, he was created baron de Clifford. He was again with Edward I at the siege of Caerlaverock Castle, 1300, distinguishing himself greatly, and these and other services prompted the next king, Edward II, to grant him Skipton castle and lands in Yorkshire taking up much of the area called Craven, many thousands of fertile acres. One 'service' was to join with a little gang of high nobles to hunt down and kill the king's favourite, Piers Gaveston, for which Robert had the king's rather forced pardon.

Robert thought Skipton a more civilised and possibly safer place to live than the Scots-threatened extremities of Westmoreland, so the Cliffords moved there and set about improving the castle. At this point was the condition written that the Clifford estates would pass down to the children, sex unspecified.

Robert had only been at Skipton two years when the call to duty came again, this time following the foolish and wayward Edward II to Bannockburn, 1314, where the Scots of Robert the Bruce won the battle and killed the 1st baron de Clifford.

The 2nd baron, another Roger, joined the duke of Lancaster's rebellion against his father's patron, Edward II, and was taken in the spring of 1322 at the Battle of Boroughbridge, so severely wounded that he was considered a dead man. One story has him surviving his wounds and living on while all the other leaders were executed; otherwise, he was hanged at York castle, his head cut off and his body hung in chains from the keep. This may be why that keep is known as Clifford's Tower, but more probably the name came about later, when the Clifford family became hereditary constables of the castle and were responsible for repairs to it.

However and whenever he died, Roger had his estates removed from him for his treachery, but they were restored to his younger brother, Robert, a peaceable kind of man given to hunting and castle restoration, and remarkable chiefly for being a male Clifford who died of natural causes.

His son, Robert, 4th baron, reasserted the previous custom. Married at sixteen or thereabouts into the great northern family of Nevilles, he set off more or less immediately for service in France with Edward III, fought at the Battle of Crécy, and was killed in another fight aged about twenty. His brother, Roger, 5th baron, although spending plenty of time in arms against the Scots, lived to be fifty-six and a grandfather, expanding Brougham castle and serving as high sheriff of both Cumberland and Westmoreland. With Maud Beauchamp, daughter of the earl of Warwick, he had five children who lived to adulthood, one of whom was neither a Roger nor a Robert but a Thomas, and something of a madcap.

Bannockburn had signalled a century and more of disturbances in the Borders. Although the Cliffords had the Eden valley *ex de* Viteripont, under control by now, they were not proof against the Scots, and on 26 December 1388, the newly prosperous market and county town of Appleby was destroyed, as was Brougham castle on the same raid.

Meanwhile, Sir Thomas liked to issue challenges to other knights and was quite happy to travel abroad for the tourney. He was favoured at court by King Richard II but fell out and was banished. His combative nature was responsible for his death at about the age of twenty-eight, whichever story you believe: either he fell ill on a pilgrimage of self-reproach to Jerusalem after killing a man in a duel somewhere in the

Baltic region or he was killed as a mercenary with the French fighting some German rebels.

He had just had time at home to father a son, John, who succeeded to the title aged one or two, eventually married Elizabeth, daughter of the famous Henry Percy called Hotspur, served with Henry V at Harfleur and Agincourt, and was killed at the Siege of Meaux, 1422.

John's son, Thomas, 8th baron de Clifford, was also a distinguished soldier but returned from France in 1455 to be on the Lancastrian side with Henry VI and was slain at St Albans in the opening battle of the Wars of the Roses, slain indeed in single combat with the duke of York himself if we are to believe Master Shakespeare. Clifford's son, John, vowed not mere revenge but to exterminate all of the House of York, which he promised also upon the stage, in the final scene of the second part of the play of King Henry VI:

> York not our old men spares;
> No more will I their babes....
> Meet I an infant of the house of York,
> Into as many gobbets will I cut it
> As wild Medea young Absyrtus did.

This was a vow of vows. As the audience of the time was expected to know, wild Medea the sorceress was mother to Absyrtus. Seeking delay while being pursued by the father, she cut up their son and left the pieces for father to find. In such a way spread the fame of Bloody John Clifford the Butcher, and he certainly earned some of his nickname.

At the Battle of Wakefield, Henry VI's Lancastrian forces ambushed the duke of York and killed him. Shakespeare, not one to let facts spoil a good story, has John Clifford and Queen Margaret herself killing the duke between them, although she was probably away in Scotland at the time. York's head with a paper crown was sent to the city of York for display on the walls.

Meanwhile, John had heard that one of the duke's sons was hiding nearby—the young Edmund, earl of Rutland. Clifford sought the boy, or rather young man of seventeen, and found him fleeing on a riverside path. Edmund knelt before him, asking for mercy. Clifford cried 'By God's blood, thy father slew mine and so will I thee, and all thy kin' and had Rutland's head added for viewing at the gallery at York. Again, this story is disputed; some (including Lady Anne herself) say that Rutland simply died in the battle in the ordinary way.

Those who live by the sword shall perish by it, and John did a year later in a skirmish before the Yorkist victory at Towton. As Shakespeare put it in the third part of *King Henry VI*:

> From off the gates of York fetch down the head,
> Your father's head, which Clifford placed there;
> Instead whereof let his supply the room.

Now the family's fortunes were dipped deep in mire. The act of attainder was passed by parliament and it was used to attaint the dead Butcher by the Yorkists, which is to say that the Clifford estates, rights, and capacities were forfeit and nothing could be inherited from Baron John. He was translated into a never-was.

A daughter, Elizabeth, married into the Aske family, and her son, Sir Robert Aske, a leader of the religious rebellion against Henry VIII known as the Pilgrimage of Grace, was hanged in chains from the walls of Clifford's Tower. A brother, Sir Roger, was executed on Tower Hill on orders from King Richard III.

The Butcher's sons, Henry (aged seven) and Richard (aged four), were liable to pay for their father's Lancastrian sins, so wife Margaret hid them at her parental home, Londesborough, in the Yorkshire Wolds, perhaps intending to ship them onwards to the continent. If so, only Richard went; according to most sources, he died in the Netherlands quite young, although he may have lived quietly in Norfolk.

Elder brother Henry stayed at Londesborough for a while, not with his mother but living as the son of a local shepherd, until his mother remarried, around 1467, to a Cumberland lord, Sir Lancelot Threlkeld of Yanwath. The legend has it that Henry, now about fourteen years old, went to live with another shepherd family in that area, near Keswick, until the Lancastrian Henry VII defeated Yorkist Richard III at Bosworth Field, 1485, and soon after restored all estates to the loyal Cliffords.

No one can be certain how much truth there is in the romantic story of the incognito tenth baron as lowly shepherd, illiterate until he was twenty-four years old, but he was given the nickname the 'Shepherd Lord' and he did follow a country life thereafter; he went up to London and the court only when called to take his seat in parliament, otherwise spending his time at Barden Tower, which had been a hunting lodge for Skipton castle but which he remodelled into a comfortable residence with an observatory after developing a great interest in astronomy and its then sister science astrology. He is alleged to have seen in the stars the end of the male line of Cliffords with his great-grandsons, which is what happened of course.

Baron Clifford the Shepherd married a noblewoman from Bedford, Anne St John of Bletsoe, and she produced seven daughters and two sons before she died aged about forty-five. His second wife, Florence, widow of Sir Thomas Talbot of Bolton, bore several sons who died in infancy and one daughter, Dorothy, who married into another powerful northern family, the Lowthers.

Henry Clifford held the North of England for King Henry, and he held it long. At the age of sixty, he commanded troops at Flodden, 1513, where the Scots were slaughtered, including their king, James IV. In 1521, his Christmas festivities were at Brough castle, where a fire broke out and left the place in ruins, and in 1523, this remarkably different Clifford died in his bed aged seventy.

The Shepherd's son, the 11th Baron Clifford, another Henry, did go to court as a young man and became a great friend of his contemporary Prince Henry, who, soon after becoming King Henry VIII, created his companion earl of Cumberland and later knight of the garter, lord president of the North of England, and lord warden of the marches. The new earl married two Margarets, the first dying not long after the wedding. The second, daughter of another Henry Percy, earl of Northumberland, brought with her a large piece of the Vale of Craven as her dowry.

Their son, Henry again, 12th baron and 2nd earl, inherited in 1542, by which time he was married to Eleanor Brandon, daughter of the duke of Suffolk and granddaughter of Henry VII, and seventh in line to the throne. It was a wedding of note; Henry VIII was there, and the expenses were so huge that the earl had to sell a rich manor in Hereford to pay for it, which was the last of the original Clifford castle estate.

Both their sons died in infancy, but their daughter, Margaret Clifford, lived to take her place in the line of succession when her mother died in 1547, the same year Henry VIII died.

That Henry's son, Edward VI, would succeed was never in doubt, but when he died childless, he wanted to prevent his sister, Mary, from returning the country to Catholicism and so named one further up the list than Margaret, Lady Jane Grey. The nine-day queen was executed on the orders of Mary who took the throne. Margaret may have harboured ambitions but, unhappily married to the earl of Derby and kept largely under house arrest by the queen, ended her life in debt and discredit.

Eleanor died in 1547 at Skipton, and Henry married again five or so years later to Anne, daughter of Lord Dacre. The family was aptly named, having something like 120,000 acres in estates across the north. Henry was a scientist and studied widely, with a great library of books, in manuscript as well as print; he and Anne had five children, three girls—two of whom died young—and two boys. In the year Queen Elizabeth came to the throne, 1558, was born son and heir, George, at Brougham castle, and a year later, his brother, Francis.

These, and Francis's son, Henry, were the last of the direct line. So, there you have the Cliffords, and a feisty lot they were. The inheritor of all that Clifford spirit was Lady Anne.

3

The Highs and Lows of Youth

When Lady Anne was born at Skipton, her father was in England but detained at court by having to give account of his voyages to Queen Elizabeth. When he did get up to Yorkshire to see his new daughter, she was eight weeks old, and within a few days, the earl had organised his family, then including the boy, Robert, to travel to London. Lady Anne would not be at Skipton again until 1649, with King Charles I beheaded and parliament in charge.

As was so often the way, a lack of sons was considered mainly the woman's fault. When the two Clifford heirs died young and there appeared no more save for Lady Anne, the parents grew apart, the earl of Cumberland and the countess—he to his adventures and his mistresses, she to a kind of single-motherhood.

Lady Anne was fourteen months old when her brother, Robert, died, and thereafter, she spent much of her early life staying with relatives in various country houses. An assiduous parent—in her daughter's words, 'a most affectionate dear and excellent mother'—the countess took steps to ensure a thorough and wide-ranging education for little Anne, not always something given top priority for girls in those days. She engaged as tutor a historian who was making a name for himself by his poetry, Samuel Daniel.

His work, which would later include a Clifford-related romance *The Complaynt of Rosamund*, would not find many modern readers other than literary historians, and his contemporaries had their opinions too. Ben Jonson said that he was an honest man but no poet; Lady Anne's father apparently said that whenever he had a wakeful night, he only had to have someone read to him a verse or two of Sam Daniel's poem and he needed no sleeping draught.

The poem he was meaning was probably the one praising his wife, the countess, which, after many tedious verses, mentioned her and trudged on with many more verses after. Or, there was the poem addressed to Lady Anne, in which he bid her fill her mind with rich furniture:

> To make ye highly good as highly born,
> And set your virtues equal to your kind.
> Such are your holy bounds, who must convey
> (If God so please) the honourable blood
> Of Clifford and of Russell, led aright
> To many worthy stems.

The furniture in question was indeed rich and would now be considered very hard going for a young girl—the writings of St Augustine, the complete works of Ovid—with light relief in the poetry of Chaucer and Spenser. Lady Anne also had a dancing master and studied music and probably French. She much revered her old teacher, Daniel, and years later, she had a monumental inscription made to him in the church of his home village. There was also a governess, Mrs Taylour, who would have studied the Bible with Lady Anne, but there was none of the most basic learning of those times for boys, instruction in Latin and Greek. This was on her father's orders; there was clearly a limit to what was seemly and proper for a female to know. This is what Lady Anne later had to say in the matter: 'The said young lady was not admitted to learn any language, because her father would not permit it, but for all other knowledge fit for her sex, none was bred up to greater perfection than herself'.

Even so, it is hard to believe that a society lady like her would be without any French, even if she could not read Montaigne's *Essays* in the original. She would not have questioned her father's edict, beyond perhaps wishing to herself that she might be allowed to study where she wanted.

> 1 Corinthians XIV xxxiv&v: Let your women keep silence in the churches, for it is not permitted unto them to speak. If they will learn any thing, let them ask their husbands at home: for it is a shame for women to speak in the church.

In any case, her health was always a concern, and she was often sent away to the fresh air of Northamptonshire to stay with her now elderly great aunt, Alice, Lady Elmes. When she was judged well enough, she came home to a house of her mother's, out in the countryside at Clerkenwell Green, rather than her mother's main residence in the city at Austin Friars (today between Old Broad Street and Moorgate), but it was from the latter that Lady Anne's social life began. At the age of twelve, she was taken up to court at Whitehall by her aunt, the countess of Warwick, where she soon became a favourite, cutting a fine figure, set to be a beauty, and an heiress to boot. Surely this last of the Cliffords was marked for an important place close to the queen, and there was talk of preferment to a place in the Privy Chamber, but soon after, the queen fell ill and moved to Richmond.

The world turned upside down in March 1603 when Lady Anne was aged thirteen and Queen Elizabeth aged sixty-nine. Aunt Warwick's servant brought the news to Austin Friars that the queen had died. There was to be a proclamation at Cheapside, and Lady Anne went out to see and hear King James VI of Scotland being claimed King James I of England, without the civil upsets and objections that many had predicted.

With the countesses of Cumberland and Warwick in attendance, the queen's body was brought on a barge from Richmond to Whitehall, where it was to lie in state, watched over by these ladies and others but not by Lady Anne, because her father had said no. She was too young, and there was more hurt yet when she was adjudged not tall enough to walk in the funeral procession. Regardless, she got herself in to the service and 'stood in the church at Westminster to see the Solemnities performed'.

By this time, father and mother were really estranged and hardly on speaking terms. The earl's dalliances with certain gentlewomen were common knowledge and hardly anything to startle in a small world where such news was no more than salt to the meat. Even so, he felt obliged to excuse himself by implying that the countess had lessened her interest in him as a man.

This was both dishonourable and incredible, the countess being two years his junior and always the dutiful wife—and people said so. This was Cumberland and Clifford, the pirate who took Puerto Rico, a man with a man's predilections for variety and an adventurer's search for new excitements. That he found it necessary to justify his *amorettes* perhaps implies a sentiment he had rather not admit.

He had been coming occasionally to Clerkenwell, and he was paying for the house, but his 'unhappy unkindnesses ... was a time of great sorrow to my saintlike Mother,' as Lady Anne put it later. Above all, though, his attentions lay with ensuring his own position with the new king.

This king came south initially without his queen, Anne of Denmark, the young princes, Henry and Charles, and the princess, Elizabeth, who were in a separate procession behind. Cumberland met King James at York with a great showing, and he carried the sword of state before him and sought favour again when he set up a splendid banquet at his temporary country residence, Grafton Regis Manor in Northamptonshire, where King James's and Queen Anne's entourages all met up. The house was once a favourite resort of Henry VIII but fell out of favour soon after this great occasion and would be burned to the ground by parliamentary forces in 1643.

Among the queen's train were Lady Margaret and her daughter, Lady Anne; the host at Grafton was the earl, but his wife was not acknowledged as mistress of the house, 'by reason', Lady Anne said, 'of the difference between my Lord and her, which was grown to a great height.' Neither could the earl's new love be acknowledged before the king and queen, so Lady Margaret just kept quiet and out of the way.

Mother and daughter stayed with Queen Anne, moving to Windsor and Hampton Court, and later to various great houses. The king chose his queen's ladies-in-waiting, but she chose differently, insisting on her own preferences and so ending up with both; she had so many that the Privy Chamber was hardly privy any more. Lady Anne was one of the select few who were not so recruited and was glad of it.

Her father, while keeping all appearances and duties in public, privately admitted doubts regarding this new king. He was not royal enough, by which was meant in his dress and bearing he lacked the regal presence and authority of Elizabeth, and his coarse speech was all the more obtrusive for his never-ending discourse on every subject under the sun, with and without matter.

It was also true that the queen was taller than he, which was the subject of speculation before the coronation at Westminster, but that curiosity was nothing compared to the whispering caused when Lady Anne and everyone there saw that the queen, being a papist converted from protestant, would not take communion from the archbishop.

In the two years following the death of Elizabeth, the court had changed greatly. Elizabeth had been guided in her politic by such as the lords of Walsingham and of Burghley—prudent, steady, pious, ever watchful for the queen's welfare and her purse, while, for her amusement, she had had the most handsome, witty, and fine-mannered men to pay court to her. When these handsome men became ambitious and attempted to stray into the glittering provinces of power, the queen always pulled them back or cleverly allowed them to engineer their own downfall.

King James also preferred the most handsome, witty, and fine-mannered men and allowed them to stray into various provinces, including his purse, which was ever open. As for the prudence of ministers, that had become less important because England was now blessed, in the view of no lesser a person than the king himself, with a king of such inexpressible wisdom that better he had ministers who were inclined to the lighter side, that they may cheer the king, so burdened was he with affairs of state. If they were frivolous and like ladies at the masque, why, so much the happier, to lift care from the king's shoulders and the heavy grey cloth of government from his back.

There were great changes on the way too in the Clifford family. The mighty earl had begun to fade. Rather pitifully, he remembered his love for his wife and regretted their enmity, but his will was planned and his thoughts advanced on a husband for Lady Anne.

The will would leave all the estates to the earl's brother, Francis, and thence to his son, Henry. In the (surely unlikely) event of no male issue maturing from this Clifford line, the estates would eventually revert to Lady Anne. The legality of this will was highly questionable; although the title of earl of Cumberland had to descend through the males, there was no such stricture on the estates or, for that matter, the barony. Being the sole heir, Lady Anne would automatically become the baroness de Clifford and, by rights, would inherit everything of the Cliffords regardless of noble titles.

As something of a sop, the will specified a purse of £15,000 to be left to Lady Anne (about £3 million today), particularly so that she remained a sound proposition for a gentleman to woo. Her father would not have her go to a 'lord of this' or an 'earl of that' with a bowl in her hands, especially as many of the very finest of such had spent their money on gentlemen's pursuits and so proffered a bowl of their own.

It was not precisely specified in the will where this £15,000 was to come from, nor how it was to be paid and by whom. Cousin Edward, Lord Wotton, brother Sir Francis Clifford, and his man John Taylor were named as responsible for paying Lady Anne's 'portion', but they were also charged with clearing the debts that encumbered the estates to the point of bankruptcy. These were tasks beyond any kind of timely achievement. Great lords like Cumberland could make such grand gestures in their wills and so die at peace, but in the event, Lady Anne's money never did appear.

The Westmoreland estates were to be the countess's jointure (hers while she lived). If that were not sufficient a blow to Anne and her mother, when it came to husbands, in law and practice, the earl could marry his daughter to whomsoever he wished. In reality, he would consult wife and daughter and, hopefully, take their views into account. Other parties might also express an interest; in a marriage of this social importance, the king himself would also have an opinion and, perhaps, a favourite of his own.

4

A Death and a Match

At the start of 1605, care had yet to press upon Lady Anne, she being but a girl of fifteen years, though she was soon to find that events can demand that a girl become a woman in spirit. We cannot know when her physical change took place, but we can be sure about the accepted wisdom concerning it.

It was widely believed that a young woman could take the smallest portion of her period, her monthly flowers, mix it with the food of a desired male, and so bewitch him into being her slave. Lady Anne would have been too educated for such nonsense, but if she had asked a physician why she had this leakage come upon her, with a pain in the belly, the reply would have been that it was because God had ordered it.

This being the same reason as everything else in the world, an inquisitive mind might have pressed for further explanations. One such was that the man had no need of this unhappy bloodletting because his blood was used to the full with his activities, whereas the woman acquires a surplus through her natural lack of activity, which oversupply has to be released as her flowers by the month, or she would fall into fits.

Other scholars claimed that men had a kind of purifying action within them that women did not have, a natural cleansing process, which was God's gift to the male sex only, and so women had to rid themselves of certain impurities by their monthly means.

Further, a woman's flowers may increase times over from small beginnings, or they may not so much. If the flow was poor, she may store up the blood within her and become sick with it. These mother fits, as they were called, caused vapours to rise from the womb into the brain and all manner of ills could result. The blood would need to be let out with the knife, or a cure may be made with herbs.

On the other hand, rich food and wine may bring about an excess in the flow, a flow of good red blood, which in turn may bring about the greensickness (later known as chlorosis or hypochromic anaemia, an iron deficiency easily treated). The only cure for the greensickness, or virgin's disease, was marriage, which was to say pregnancy. A woman with child does not give her flowers, of course, and so the inundation dries up and the greensickness with it.

With such thoughts, of exchanging the greensickness for the very real perils of childbirth, Lady Anne might have been well advised to send for her maid and have her bring a sillery bub, made with new milk, sack (wine), sugar, and lemon—considered the ideal sustenance for one in a newly flowered state.

While her mother consulted lawyers on the subject of the will, Lady Anne had to keep her wits about her as theoretical queues formed of potential suitors. At fifteen years old, strong and blossoming, something of a beauty, connected to every great family in the land including the king's, and child of one of the most famous men in England, how many young women would not have leaped into her place if they could, and how many of the eligible young men of our country would be standing in line when the time came?

Such matters would have to wait, as events overtook all plans. In the summer of 1605, Lady Anne, having lately had little close contact with the earl, was summoned to Grafton Regis to stay with him there for a month. The countess was not greatly in favour but there was no denying their lord. It is possible that he felt some guilt about the will, although showing no signs of changing it, and guilt about his estrangement from the countess, although likewise doing little but expressing his sincere wishes.

During Lady Anne's stay at Grafton, as well as walks with her father, they hunted several times each week, but the earl excused himself from time to time, complaining of a mild sickness that was insufficient to seek the advice of a physician. That was a matter not mentioned in a letter written from Grafton at the end of August, addressed to the 'Right Honourable and very good Lady and Mother, the Countess of Cumberland', in which the daughter says that her father would not have her follow the progress of the court to Oxford but she would meet it there on the morrow.

> ... after my being there, I will send my footman to your Ladyship, that you may know how things go with me, for I have had a great deal of talk with my Lord about that matter you know of, for that match, and my Lord hath promised me that there shall nothing pass for any match whatsoever, but that your consent should be asked as a chief matter.

Lady Anne's treat at the house of her father came to an end, with nothing said about the will and nothing done about it. The earl escorted her to London and through the town to Blackheath and on her way to where her mother was staying for a while by Shooter's Hill.

If the earl knew within himself that it was near too late to change the will in any case, he did not show it then, in the August, but by October, he was feeling so ill that a return to London could not be contemplated and was writing this from Grafton:

> Sweet and Dear Meg,
> Bear with, I pray thee, the short and unapt setting together of these my last lines, a token of true kindness, which I protest cometh out of an unfeigned heart of love to thee, for whose content, and to make satisfaction for the wrongs done to thee, I have, since I saw thee, more desired to return than for any other earthly cause, but being so low brought as that, without God's miraculous favour there is no great likelihood of it ... and further I beg of thee that thou wilt take, as I have meant, in kindness, the course I have set down for the disposing of my estate ... and in the nearest love of my heart I desire thee, to take great care of that sweet Nan, whom God bless, may be carefully brought up in the fear of God, not to delight in worldly vanities, which I too well know be the baits to draw her out of the Heavenly Kingdom ... begging thy pardon for any wrong that ever in my life I did thee.... Thine as wholly as ever man was woman's, George Cumberland.

By God's miracle or not, he did come back to London and took to his bed at the old Duchy House, so called because it was the duke of Lancaster's, hard by the Savoy Hospital on the Strand. No physician, and there were many called to him, could identify the ague from which he suffered, nor offer any remedy or palliative. The mighty earl of Cumberland shook, sweated, and shrank before his watchers' eyes, and he cried out in pain and nothing could be done of any use.

Knowing he would soon be taken, he resorted to belabouring his faithful wife and daughter, by his constant side, with pleas and enjoinments, buffeting them one day with piteous requests, such as not to defy God's will by grieving over much, and another day with directives in the matter of his will. The countess would do as he bid, that being her nature, at least as far as her daughter's virtue was concerned.

They were also asked to try to think better of the earl's brother, Francis, for the will was not of his doing, and they may have thought it may not be his doing, but it would certainly not be his undoing. He would be mighty glad of it and could not be expected to give Lady Anne's inheritance back, no matter how much better he was thought of.

This champion of a great queen, this scourge of the Spaniard, became a shell, his hair almost gone, his beard like a wisp of old hay, his frame hardly strong enough to hold itself together. The countess grieved silently and with her own strength, and though resolved not to hinder the immediate execution of the will as it then appeared, she was doubly resolved to discover the legal sand on which it was built. Later, Lady Anne recorded the last moments:

> My noble and brave father died in the Duchy house by the Savoy at London near the River of Thames when he was about three months past forty seven years old. My Mother and I being present with him at his death, I being then just fifteen years and nine months old. When a little before his death he expressed with much affection to my Mother and me, and a great belief that he had that his brother's son would die without issue male, and thereby all his Lands would come to be mine.

The Rt Hon. earl of Cumberland, knight of the garter, Baron Clifford, baron and sheriff of Westmoreland, lord of the honour of Skipton *et cetera*, born at Brougham Castle in Westmoreland, which was of the Cliffords since 1270, was buried at Skipton.

> 2 Samuel I ixx: The beauty of Israel is slain upon thy high places. How are the mighty fallen.

Clifford's reasons for making that will cannot be known. He seemed to be regretting it at the end, but he took no action. Perhaps he really believed that the estates should go with the greater title, the earldom, which Anne could not have, and so keep the males of the family at the top of society.

Perhaps he hoped that his very wealthy and prudent brother would be able to sort out at least some of the debts and mortgages left behind and return the Clifford lands to stability and profit.

Regardless of the earl's beliefs and wishes, the fact remained—not entirely or immediately appreciated by Lady Anne and her mother—that the barony de Clifford passed to the daughter on her father's death and with it the lands associated. Whatever might be the arguments about earldoms and the Yorkshire estates, granted to the Cliffords without specification of heirs to be male, by the law of the land, Westmoreland came with the barony and was Lady Anne's from that moment.

While the countess was determined to pursue the case through the law courts, she knew that matters were unlikely to be resolved that way, despite all the papers, historical precedent, and the many, many hours of study undergone by squadrons of lawyers. In particular, she was resolute that the Westmoreland estates, her jointure in life, should not revert to her brother-in-law on her death, but would come to Lady Anne. For this, too, she realised, she would have to plead before the king.

> Matthew XXIII xxiii: Woe unto you, scribes, and Pharisees, hypocrites, for ye pay tithe of mint and anise and cumin, and have omitted the weightier matters of the law, judgement, mercy, and faith.

Great suits in law involving important people, with learned lawyers on both sides arguing, tended to end up in front of the king for his judgement, all reinforced by the almost universal opinion that a woman should always be subservient to a man and a wife should obey her husband without question in every instance. Therefore, it might be held that the countess had no business going against her late husband's wishes.

Perhaps a more moderate view could sometimes be found in Lady Anne's time that the husband had precedence but also responsibility; he should be considerate of his wife and should consult and be advised by his wife in those instances where she could have useful knowledge. If such a change were to continue and not be halted, then by logic the day would come when women stood equal with men.

Meanwhile, in reality, the authorities stated that God created woman out of man after He created man; therefore, the man is the better of the two. Eve was weak, gave in to temptation, ate the forbidden fruit, and so caused the downfall of Adam and mankind, therefore, the man is the better of the two. Man is naturally of the hot and dry humours but woman is, naturally, a creature of the cool and the damp, therefore, the man is the better of the two. Therefore, while the man who toiled in the fields must bow before such persons as Lady Anne because of her rank, she must acknowledge his manly powers beyond her understanding and must seek his aid should she be threatened by a shower of rain or a stone in her shoe.

The earl had been a fearless champion, but his widow and daughter knew men who were cowardly and men who were drawn not to women but to other men, some among the very highest in the land who hardly made any difference between the two sexes. They knew men who spent more time adoring themselves in the glass than any woman ever did.

The countess and Lady Anne would see themselves as courageous, determined, and never to be browbeaten by men, yet the natural law stated that such a thing was not possible, for the woman was the mouse and the man was the lion. If that was so, why did the mighty and wise lion eat the fruit of the forbidden tree offered him by the mouse? Why did he not refuse it, saying 'Alas my poor wife, can you not see it is a trick?'

As to humours, well, surely the man as a rule was hotter, angrier, more ready to draw the sword, more ready to get his way by force of arms than force of argument, which was to say that might was right and, therefore, women were inferior. The question was, should that be so?

In any case, said the men, if Lady Anne were to inherit, she would only take all her estates into her marriage to become her husband's and their children's thereafter, so what was all the fuss about?

The first matter to attend to after her father's death was the question of Anne's wardship. An underage heir whose father died was liable to become the king's ward, which gave the crown rights on a proportion of the inherited estate's income until the ward reached the age of twenty-one for males and fourteen for females. In such a case, the king would also assume the late father's rights in the question of his ward's marriage.

Lady Anne was past the age where there was any financial interest for a royal guardian, and her petition to the Court of Wards for her mother to become guardian was successful. This prevented her becoming an object of favour in the king's gift, and an object of trade between those who would guard her and match her to a husband at a profit to themselves. With her daughter as her proper ward, her mother had the law on her side, as well as right.

5

Talk of Suitors, and a Journey North

Preliminary manoeuvres now began in pursuit of the hand of Lady Anne. That she would marry was never in doubt, and unlike her maids, she could not choose only where her heart might lie. Ladies and gentlemen of rank and quality had their husbands and wives chosen for them. Doubtless the servant girls would have traded places and exchanged their hearts' desires for the exchequer in a lord's purse and a life free of drudgery, while a lady may have envied them their freedom to pick. Serving girls had all the years of their youth to court their loves, and as many as they might until they found the one they liked best. They may even have practised certain of the arts of love and been to fairs and feasts and high days without chaperone.

With the Lady Anne and her like, the main concern of parents, guardians, and kings was rarely for happiness nor love; it was for a good match, by which was meant one that strengthened the position of the two families. A lady might have been able to say no to one match or even two, but, being well born, with lands and gold in store, and handsome, and a cousin to the king, Lady Anne could not continue a maid *ad infinitum*.

She would have prayed that the gentleman would have had some say in the matter of whom he was to wed. A man choosing her, or helping to choose her, or influencing the choice somewhat, would have been the more acceptable than one who was told by his father that such and such was the case, and it followed that the Lady Anne Clifford would be his bride and bearer of his children.

In June 1606, the queen had a baby girl, who was christened Sophia in great haste and died the day after. This was Queen Anne's eighth child, with only three living, being the great favourite Prince Harry, the near invisible Charles, and the Princess Elizabeth, who was doubtless already matched with some foreign king-to-be. Such was the lot of high-born women, even queens. Anne of Denmark had been married unseen to King James VI of Scots, standing in her father's second kingdom, Norway, while he stood in Scotland, and so they were wed at a distance. And so, women married where the men willed, and bore children as often as may be, and saw them die if they did not die themselves.

By early 1607, Richard Sackville, Lord Buckhurst, was the most persistent of Lady Anne's suitors; there was bound to be a suspicion that his desire for her was not entirely pure, of love alone, but blended with the happy thought of her £15,000 being his. He and she were of an age, being newly seventeen, and one day he would be the earl of Dorset, but he showed signs of vices not unlike Lady Anne's late father, being inclined to wagers and those expensive sports that had become the occupation of gentlemen where there were no more worthwhile pursuits to fill their time. Looseness with money was in the Sackville family, young Richard's grandfather as Lord High Treasurer being so famously excellent at spending the king's gold that he became known as Lord Sackville of Fillsack, and was created earl of Dorset for his services to the crown.

With all that said, young Buckhurst was of a sweet nature and generous to a fault, scholarly and valiant and in all things mannered gently, and he rode a horse better than a gypsy and twice as elegant. He made a fine pair with the king's son, Prince Henry, and they were great friends together. As Lady Anne put it laconically later, he was a 'lover of scholars and soldiers as that, with an excessive bounty towards them or, indeed, any of worth, that he did much diminish his estate'. Lady Anne also pointed out that 'his mother being Lady Margaret Howard, only daughter to Thomas Duke of Norfolk, who was beheaded' (2 June 1572).

Though Lord Buckhurst was in the lead, there was still much jousting and feinting and conspiring around the hand of Lady Anne. Even without her estates, she was a catch indeed, and there was always the possibility that the estates might accrue too. For Lady Anne, there was much more sport to come but, before that, there was to be an adventure of a quite different kind. The dowager countess had decided that her jointure was to be visited and surveyed, and Lady Anne, who might one day be queen of all of it, should accompany her. The journey began in the early summer of 1607.

Exact details of the route are not known, but the options were few. A useful network of decent inns (no such thing as a hotel) had yet to be established; there were not the numbers of travellers to justify hospitality as a trade, nor were there good roads for them to travel on. If a local stretch of road was well made and maintained, there would be a reason, such as it leading to an important person's house.

The countess and Lady Anne would have had several four-horse coaches to carry their maids and other staff, plus outriders, and they would be expecting to stay with other noble families on their way. Their first target would normally have been Theobalds, a great house near Cheshunt built by Lord Burleigh and much visited by Queen Elizabeth, now in the hands of Burleigh's son, the new earl of Salisbury, but this was in the process of being transferred to the king, he liking it better than his other house nearby at Hatfield, which he was swapping. Salisbury was not in there yet, so neither place was available.

The ladies' first day must therefore have been a long one, leaving the countess's house in Austin Friars, turning into Broad Street and Bishop's Gate and on up the main road from the capital to the north (the Roman road Ermine Street, now partly the A10), past the villages of Tottenham and Edmonton and on towards Ware. There was an acceptable inn just off their way, the White Horse at Hertingfordbury, and they may have stayed there.

A logical next stop would have been Knebworth, home of Sir Rowland Lytton, whom both ladies had known at Queen Elizabeth's court where he was captain of the Band of Gentleman Pensioners. Next day, after Royston, there could have been good progress on the long, straight way to Hinchingbrooke House at Huntingdon, where Sir Oliver Cromwell, cousin to another Oliver Cromwell, lived and where King James had stayed on his way south. Other stops for the ladies could have been Burghley, and with an old friend, Sir Thomas Meres, at Aubourn Hall near Lincoln. Sir Thomas was a country gentleman of the old sort and, far from the tricks and deceits of court, lived a simple life. The nearer they were to Skipton and Appleby, perhaps they thought the more simple life should be. Another two days could have taken them to Bawtry, Doncaster, Pontefract, and Temple Newsham near Leeds, birthplace of their cousin, Lord Darnley, father of King James.

Skipton castle was their first objective, and to get there they would pass the strangest part of a road, through Leeds to the abbey at Kirkstall. This, like many abbeys, had been a rich and thriving place, almost a town unto itself, until King Henry VIII dissolved it. Like many, it was stripped bare of valuables such as roof lead, but not laid flat. To prevent the monks coming back, the road was diverted through the abbey church, so that the ladies' coaches went beneath the arch of what had been the east window as if it were a bar in a city wall, and on down the nave that, being paved with flat stone, was the best piece of road on the whole of their march, and out by the great west door.

Matters fell out at Skipton not as hoped but as expected. They were met beyond the castle gate by Lady Anne's uncle, Francis Clifford, newly earl of Cumberland, and his son, her cousin, Henry. The earl said they should not be granted entry as the quarrel over their inheritances was *sub judice*. Lady Margaret asked how that could be, since the case was yet in no court of law, and that simple hospitality for a wayfarer was a duty, and that a beggar at the gate could expect more than they had been offered.

If the earl wavered before his sister-in-law, Henry was strong against and was the steel in Francis's back, speaking hotly; they would have been turned away entirely if the better nature of the earl had not prevailed. They were given a guide who took them a little further along the road and up a hill track to a farm that had a pleasant house, and the people there stayed in a barn and the ladies had the house.

Lady Margaret was having an alms-house built for poor widows at Beamsley, just nearby, so they looked at that before pressing on to their final destination, the lands of Lady Margaret's jointure in Westmoreland. As they left Skipton behind, Lady Anne may have listened to her mother's tale of the Barguest, the black hound of Craven, big as a wild fell horse with eyes the size of a man's hand, and of the many boggarts, goblins, and other demons that attended the beast in Troller's Gill, near to the Barden Tower, built by the Shepherd Lord. This Barguest could appear at will, anywhere, and was a sign of death to any who saw it or felt its burning breath upon them, and no person from any place near Trollerdale, not even the holy men of Bolton Abbey, would ever go into the Gill at night nor would they go alone in the day. One day, Lady Anne might be mistress of Barden; would she go?

The road to Kirkby Lonsdale was in a poor state and largely unsuitable for a carriage, and beyond was worse, as they turned for Sedbergh and were plunged into a wild land, at first following a river valley with high hills to their right, and then they had such a climb up and beyond Sedbergh that they thought their horses might die of the effort, and then down, and then up, and then up again, in among the mountains called How Gills, across rivers, and lowering upon them was the great mountain or Fell called Wild Boar.

The story goes that one day a monk was crossing this Fell, who was famous for his sermons that were so dusty, dry, and bereft of the slightest curiosity that entire congregations were put to sleep moments after he opened his mouth. This monk was carrying with him a roll of parchment on which he had composed his newest sermon and, when a wild boar came at him, his sermon was his only weapon. He thrust it down the throat of the boar whereupon it closed its eyes, slept, and died of thirst. And that is how the Fell had its name.

At last they descended into a green valley and could see the ruinations of the castle at Mallerstang, called Pendragon, and the village of Kirkby Stephen looked well enough. They went through Musgrave and Warcop, and crossed the bridge into Appleby. They made Appleby castle their place of residence, though it had been much despoiled in the rebellion of the catholic earls against Elizabeth. There remained sufficient accommodation for their needs, and room too for the local wrongdoers who were kept there ready for the visiting judges of the assizes.

The plan was to visit all the castles belonging to the barony. They did not expect closer inspection to reveal much of use or ornament at Brough, which needed work, nor at Pendragon, which was almost too far gone for restoration. Brougham, where Lady Anne's father was born, was also imperfect but fit to be set right without too great an expense, and Lady Margaret was determined it should be restored, and she expected to live there when Lady Anne was wed and householded.

> Isaiah XXXV i: The wilderness and the solitary place shall be glad for them; and the desert shall rejoice, and blossom as the rose.

Lady Margaret wished to have herself seen as the dowager countess and rightful owner, and to put herself and Lady Anne in the minds of the people. Lady Anne's first viewing of her inheritance made a powerful impression, one which would govern her life. Even so, once returned to London, other matters were afoot. Castles and inheritances could be forgotten when affairs of the heart were pressing.

6

Another Suitor, a Masque, and a Match

The grandfather of suitor-in-chief Lord Buckhurst died suddenly while seated at the king's Privy Council table. This was Thomas, earl of Dorset, a famous man who did many great services for Queen Elizabeth (whose cousin he was) and for England. If he was something profligate with King James's treasury when he would better have reined in their majesties from their natural lavishness, he was only doing their will. Dorset it had been who conveyed in person to Queen Mary of Scots, King James's mother, the news that her life was to end on the block.

The elder son, Robert, learned and scholarly, succeeded him, which made Lord Buckhurst the earl of Dorset-in-waiting and Lady Anne, should she choose to follow the advice of half the world, the countess to come. But now into the picture came another suitor with little rank at all.

Everywhere at court, Sir Robert Kerr seemed to pop up. He may have been the king's favourite, but he was not Lady Anne's, handsome though he was and able to turn the heads of other young girls. To him, life was a jest with no space for intellectual activity. The spirit of youth can be a fine thing, but he was the same age as Lady Anne, who had her serious side.

There was pressure from the top, when the king sounded Lady Margaret on the subject of a match between her daughter and Kerr. Here was Lady Anne Clifford, daughter of an earl and of the royal line, descendant of King Henry VII's daughter, near an old maid at eighteen and so like to take her fortune with her to the grave, while this most eligible of Scots was without a bawbee to his name that the king did not give him. For an instance, the king gave young Master Kerr the manor of Sherborne, which was Sir Walter Ralegh's, who was in the Tower at the time.

Sir Robert was the youngest son of a Scottish baron of the Marches, Sir Thomas Kerr, who did great service to the king's mother, Queen Mary of Scots. While this may have been sufficient for the king to give young Kerr preferment, it was not the only reason. He was a page boy when the king came south and the Scots had him picked for a favourite, and somehow he became a groom of the royal bedchamber and a knight, and there he was the apple of the king's eye. In his dress and manners, he became most affected, so that the king showered his love upon him as if he were Lady Kerr, whereupon this gallant fell from his horse and broke his leg.

The countess of Suffolk, a cousin to Lady Anne, had been much pressed by the English lords to find an English favourite for the king, to take his mind away from the boy Kerr. The countess had been most assiduous, preparing many handsome young men with all her arts of appearance, with perfume and curling the hair, but all her hopes were dashed with Kerr's fall. Now the king was like a mother with a sick child, or a husband with a bride in her first childbearing, and the more the king sought to succour Sir Robert, the more the fawning lords of court did the same, until those same English lords who had so prevailed upon Lady Suffolk to produce a flower from her garden now gathered at the bedside of the Scots' own flower, with sweetmeats and all manner of gifts, until the king was minded to order restraint that so much of a throng of well-wishers was having the opposite effect. Lady Anne, notwithstanding, kept her glance upon her own preferences.

In February 1609, her match was fixed to Lord Buckhurst, betrothed, promised, assured, contracted, and vowed, and all other schemes, whether the king's or not, could be forgotten, or so it seemed. Young Buckhurst professed his love and devotion, and Lady Anne was happy, but before minds could concentrate on all the great arrangements needed for the wedding of the year, there was a diversion.

Lady Anne was to dance in one of Ben Jonson's masques, called *The Masque of Queens*, which had witches played by professional actors and twelve queens, played by Queen Anne herself and eleven ladies of the court. Lady Anne was to play Queen Berenice of Egypt. In pursuit of dramatic accuracy, Master Jonson could have given Lady Anne to understand that her Berenice was not the one who was sister to Cleopatra and who was put to death, nor the one who was murdered three weeks after marrying King Alexander, nor the one who was the daughter of Salome, remarkable in this company for living to the end of her days without their being violently shortened.

Lady Anne was to be the Berenice who cut off her hair, which was apt since she was famous for her hair that reached to the calves of her legs. Her husband, King Ptolemy, being away on a military campaign, had Queen Berenice's prayers for his safe return, and to ensure this, she cut off the hair and placed it in the temple as an offering. This hair, being the most wonderful hair in Egypt, was translated into the heavens where it appeared as a new constellation, *Coma Berenices*. So far so good, and King Ptolemy indeed returned safe, but when he died, Berenice's own son, the new king, murdered her.

Inigo Jones came to court with his designs for the costumes, and Lady Anne's was a rare thing. There was a mighty tall hat like a bishop's mitre but with an ostrich feather, beneath which her hair had to be dressed since she was supposed to have left it in the temple, and a flowing cloak wrapped about her in the manner of a Roman toga, and beneath it a bodice, which could not be counted as modest.

With that interlude played to great acclaim, the news came suddenly that the father of Buckhurst, the earl of Dorset, so lately in the title, was failing. Lady Margaret was quick to see to the heart of the matter. Should Lord Buckhurst have been a bachelor still at his father's death, he, not being of age, would be taken into wardship by whomsoever the king chose, and the guardian would have a free hand with the matching of his ward. This was the fate that Lady Anne herself had escaped only nearly.

The risk of the king choosing an unsuitable guardian was too great, for his mind was swayed this way and that by advisors and his decisions were often capricious. A scheme was already rumoured to be set in train by the duke of Lennox, who was of the Stuart line. The duke's plan was one in which a certain gentlewoman of Scotland, not identified by the gossips, would be given in marriage to Lord Buckhurst. This lady and his grace of Lennox would have much to gain from the match, but the lady brought little with her. There would be no fortune, few accomplishments, and only plain looks to persuade young Buckhurst that in Scotland he had the better bride, but were he a ward, he would have no say in the matter.

Lady Margaret had her own scheme: to nip the Lennox in the bud by having her daughter marry at once. This was no easy thing for a mother to do, who had lost her sons years before and her husband recently, and who had only her daughter left to her, a daughter with whom a bond had been forged in adversity. When Lady Anne became a wife and countess of Dorset, she would also be mistress of the house at Knole, in Kent, while her mother's duties lay in the north, in Westmoreland, where life was ever different from that in the easeful south. Lady Margaret would have little company of the sort she was used to, at court and at home, and would have to bear such barrenness alone.

As for Lady Anne, she would have had to come to terms with her new status in life. Any learned books on the subject were written by men, and so the only advice available was from those who had no womanly experience to bolster their learning.

First she had to understand that her marriage signified a change of ownership. From being the charge of parents or ward, the bride was given away into the charge of her husband. This husband put on the parents' coat in some ways; for example, he took upon himself the duty of chastisement, so that if the wife needed it, he would beat her. Judgement of extent of the need, and consequent amount of beating, were left to the husband.

Subjection of wife to husband was written in the laws of the land and the church, and according to custom, it had ever been so from the day Eve ate of the forbidden fruit. For a lady of Anne Clifford's temperament, she might have expected to love her husband but not to be his servant. She might have believed that a husband should be a wife's companion in life and her greatest friend, and she his, and lovers together, which were valiant thoughts for one who, defying her husband, could be beaten within an inch of her life and still within the law.

Lady Anne would have to see if her mettle and his could resolve into a true and general condition that was tolerable and pleasing to both, without rancour and strife. Compliance and deference, yes, but not servitude.

As well as beating her, the husband had another right over his wife, which was to come to her bed at any time, and she had to be agreeable. The general opinion among the wise men of the world was that, since woman was created to bear a man's children for him, she would be ever eager for conceiving and could not be satiated in pursuit of that impulse. God gave women the task of generation and so it would have been very strange, not to say ungodly, were she to be other than desperate for more and more children, even though she knew how many of her kind had found a full womb the quickest way to the grave.

Further, a married man was warned by the physicians not to allow his wife to sport him too much for, given the opportunity, this is what she would do, to the point where the man was milked dry like an old cow and fit for nothing but the butcher's hook.

Regardless of all the wisdom and nonsense that passed for wisdom, we can be sure that Lady Anne wanted a loving marriage with children, and she had every reason to suppose that that was to be her happy fate.

Misgivings, fears, excitements, and passions were mixed together and resolved upon 25 February 1609, when Lady Anne Clifford was wedded to Richard Sackville, Lord Buckhurst. There was no need to go far, the journey being from her own chamber but a few steps to her mother's chamber where the ceremonials were held under the countess's supervision. Haste cut short the company and the feastings, and they were joined in matrimony in simple fashion.

A wedding gift from the queen arrived, being a curling, twisting shell not unlike a whelk's but bigger, curiously made in silver with a diamond at its tip. The letter with it commended it as a mystery of the East, there being such shells in the oriental oceans that, when placed beneath the pillow, encouraged the conception of children. Countess Margaret wanted to know if the queen meant that such shells grew like this one, in silver with a diamond. In any case, it would be valued more for its giver and its beauty than any magic in it.

The marriage of a king's cousin with a future earl, in other circumstances, would surely have been a great occasion. As it was, time allowed only a modest celebration in the hall of the countess's house with, we believe, only a few guests. There are no records of what feast those guests enjoyed; if time had allowed, a typical menu might have featured a boar's head, with a pudding and a rich sauce, also capon and pheasant for the ladies, sturgeon, and a Lombardy custard (a kind of sweet fruit pie with bone marrow, dates, and prunes).

When sufficient representation had been made of that, it would have been taken away and the next course brought, perhaps a frumenty (porridge) with venison, a roast peacock with feathers replaced, a suckling pig, and fried brawn with vinegar. Three courses might have been the best they could manage, so the third could have had fish—perch and pike possibly—and various roast birds, pies of fruits and almonds, and many sweetmeats.

In more elaborate circumstances, with time and resources to prepare, with each course would have come a soltey, a fashion of those times soon to be considered vulgar, being an elaborated edifice of the cooks' imaginings, a dragon or a fairy castle, made of sweet paste and sugar, beribboned and bedecked, a kind of jest to delight those at dinner and to show how these cooks were brilliant stars in the sky.

Feast or no, we can be sure that one of the rituals associated with weddings was gratefully avoided. In private consummation, there would have been no crowd of relatives and well-meaning friends to assist at the bedding. Bride and groom could have prepared themselves in their own time and not like some, where they may as well have been appearing in a play of Ben Jonson's in front of groundlings, so coarse was the talk of such gentlefolk gathered in witness. And so began a new life for Lady Anne.

> Joel II xxviii: And it shall come to pass afterward, that I will pour out my spirit upon all flesh; and your sons and your daughters shall prophesy, your old men shall dream dreams, your young men shall see visions.

7

Married Life, with Disagreements and Childbirth

Lady Anne Clifford thus became Lady Buckhurst, and two days later was the countess of Dorset when her new husband's father, the 2nd earl, died. Although they had manors in four counties, the main seat of the Sackvilles was Knole, by Sevenoaks in Kent, and, after the funeral, there the Countess Anne was bound as the new mistress of a great household who, two days before, had been quite excited enough just to get married.

The dowager countess of Cumberland, her mother, Lady Margaret, was headed for Brougham castle. Lady Anne's journey was short and into abundance and comfort. Her mother's was long, to hard lands and a hard task of restoration and consolidation with money short. Her daughter had a hard task, too, but with money plentiful, at least for the moment.

Lady Anne's carriage would have crossed London Bridge into Southwark and begun her journey on the Dover road. Here she was leaving court, leaving everything she knew, going a short distance but to a life that would be a novelty entirely, where much would be expected of her. Passing through 4 miles or so of countryside after Southwark, the entourage met a town again, Deptford. This was a good road across Black Heath and over Shooter's Hill, it being important to the king that his messengers could reach Dover with no delay.

Into the forests beyond, they met the hamlet of Welling and the village of Crayford, and so to Dartford where they rested because here they must leave the Dover road and find their way by lesser paths.

Lady Anne may have thought back to her journey to Westmoreland with her dear mother two years before and how different the country was there. In the county of Kent, so busy were the folk with marketing and other trade that the paths became lanes and the lanes became roads. Everywhere were seen cattle and geese being driven to the Dartford butchers, goodwives with handcarts of eggs, winter cabbages, and cheese, wagons of the ironmasters and quarry masters, and all abustle so that it was no more easy to pass along the road in the country than in London town.

From Dartford, the way followed the course of the river Darent, and they passed through the hamlet of Sutton, remarkable for its old house built by the crusaders of the Order of St John of Jerusalem, who were displaced by King Henry VIII. Everywhere in the valley were fruit trees, naked then but promising much for the summer and autumn. At Eynsford, there was a ruined castle, and by it, Sir Percival Hart's house at Lullingstone. Shoreham and Otford rattled by, and at last they were at Sevenoaks and through it to Knole.

Lady Anne's new house was built by Cardinal Bourchier, archbishop of Canterbury, in the reign of Edward IV, on to an old fortified place more suitable for military commanders than princes of the church or countesses. It was briefly held by Archbishop Cranmer, who was prevailed upon to give it to Henry VIII. Master Cranmer tried to persuade the king to have the house at Otford instead, it being bigger, but the king liked Knole the better, which was on higher ground and so less likely to be troubled by the plague.

Cranmer still argued, because he had the same preference for Knole as did the king, so Henry's reply was to take both Knole and Otford saying that, while he was at Knole, the main part of his retinue could stay as the archbishop wished at Otford, and he would build more at Knole until it was befitting to a king. Poor Thomas Cranmer had even worse dealings from monarchs after that, when he was burned at the stake by Queen Mary for heresy, and Knole remained with the crown until 1566 when Queen Elizabeth gave it to Thomas Sackville. He was a cousin to the queen's mother, Anne Boleyn, and so to the queen herself, and the queen made him the 1st Baron Buckhurst. He was also famous as the co-author with Thomas Norton of *The Tragedie of Gorboduc*, performed in January 1562 and the first English tragedy written in blank verse.

By all accounts, the house of Knole had the finest and tallest chimneypiece to be seen anywhere, in marble and alabaster and made for Cardinal Bourchier, which was in the greatest room, and the carved screen in the hall was to be marvelled at. There were seven courtyards, one for each day of the week, and fifty-two staircases, for each week of the year, and 365 rooms. If Lady Anne asked the earl if he had confirmed these numbers with his own eyes, he may have said he had counted the courtyards.

The new countess was a Clifford and not to be trifled with. She would make herself felt in the matter of her household at Knole. Her husband could leave all to stewards and their hierarchies of servants, but that would not do for Lady Anne. In fact, for some years, it seemed that the household had been left to run itself so the countess would have sent for Master Legge, who had the name of steward there, and the earl's chief secretary, Master Caldicott. Lady Anne did not take to Matthew Caldicott as she might have to a sympathetic person, but in any case a list of the household was made.

In rounded terms, of the rank of Caldicott and Legge, such as the chaplain, the auditor, chief gentleman of horse, chief attendants on the earl and the countess, and those goodwives who were mistresses of chamber, wardrobe, and kitchen, there were twenty, and these sat to dinner at the parlour table.

Of the next rank, being such as clerk to the kitchen, cooks, pastry man, slaughter man, brewers and bakers, provisioner, yeomen of buttery and pantry, and gardeners, there were twenty more, and these sat to dinner at the clerks' table in the hall.

Of the next rank, being various attendants on the family, barber, scrivener, huntsmen, falconer, yeomen, ushers and grooms, footmen, coachmen, armourers, and other men, they had forty more who sat at the long table.

In the laundry, there was a dozen, and in the scullery, six. In addition, they had two blackamoors and a French boy, and these sat also at the long table. They had none as yet in the nursery.

Lady Anne was too fresh to her position to say if such a household of a hundred, or a greater number, was needed, or one that was differently arranged, but she would have been determined to show that she would be mistress of it. Certain questions were tempting to ask. What, for instance, was the daily work of Solomon the Bird Catcher? There would be dinners, banquets rather, where guests would expect swan, heron, curlew, and other wild birds, but surely they could be got when required, without employing a man year around. And who was idle among these, when they had only one dairymaid and yet eight footmen?

> From a Book of Comportments, regarding behaviour at dinner.
> All must sit upright and while you may cut your bread and pour your beer, you may not eat nor drink until the dinner is brought in and served. At the higher tables, once the meat is given out with the sauces, you will not bite your bread with your mouth, but break it with your fingers, for to bite it is uncivil to those below who must eat from your bread when it is passed down. Do not take into your mouth more than a few morsels at a time. Your mouth is not an ale bucket, to be filled and swilled, and you are shent for drinking with food in your mouth. Also, do not speak while you have food within your mouth, and do not make noises in your eating nor blow wind upon your food. To wipe your knife on the table's cloth is agreeable to none, nor to lean on the table with your elbows, nor to raise food to your lips with your knife but with your spoon always. Do not dip into your beer or wine with your fingers, to find a fly or no, for this is a vice. When drinking your wine, you have linen to wipe your mouth, and you must use the same before you take drink and after it. When dishes have been taken away, do not then say you want more and call them back, nor will you make loud note of what is not provided, nor ask for it. Do not spit, nor send forth any thing from your nose, nor clean any part of your person. When seated at the board, make no talk nor tale which will shame or sadden your fellows.

While Lady Anne was taking a firm grip of Knole, the king was doing the same with his kingdom, making in March 1610 a speech before parliament that caught fire among the members, some even of the noblest of them. It became the talk of the court, making mention of King John and the Magna Carta, and Julius Caesar, and much murmuring from doctors of learning about government by Athenian principles, which they called democracy, where the common people govern themselves and high officers are chosen by lot.

The king said to parliament that kings are God's lieutenants on earth and sit on God's throne, and they are justly called gods themselves for they can create or destroy, give life or death, and are accountable to none but God only. The rights of men are not rights at all, but privileges granted by a kind father—that is, the king—and his good will gives men liberty or takes it away.

Perhaps it was that truth—that kings can give life or death—which caused those who talked of tyranny, revolution, and Athens to do so most quietly, and in the end to hold their peace and agree with the king.

Judges XVII vi: In those days there was no King in Israel but every man did that which was right in his own eyes.

In June of that year, word came from France that their king, Henri-Quatre, had been assassinated by a Catholic madman. This French king said once of King James, 'He is the wisest fool in Christendom', by which was meant that King James was most knowing, or canny as he might have had it, in the details of life and its comforts, but he could not display the same abilities when the large questions were debated. Possibly, the French king had a good point, for James was very good at employing the purses of others to pay his own bills.

Now there was to be a masque, *Tethys' Festival*, as part of the greater festivals and feasts marking Henry's investiture as Prince of Wales. The author of the masque was Lady Anne's old tutor, Samuel Daniel, whose extensive curriculum had somehow missed the life and times of Tethys, so Lady Anne, the old pupil, sought out the old master and asked him to find that Tethys was a Titan, one of the first Greek gods, daughter of Uranus and Gaia, wife of Oceanus, whose endless river flows ceaselessly around the edges of the world, or at least did until the modern philosophers discovered that the world is a ball that spins around the sun.

By Oceanus, Tethys gave birth to 3,000 rivers and 4,000 water nymphs, a cast of players that Master Daniel had clipped somewhat. It seems that the thoughtful Tethys included English rivers among her progeny, she being responsible for the whole of the ancient world and not merely the Greek part, and Lady Anne was to play the River Aire, or the nymph thereof. This part was hers because she was born at Skipton Castle, on the banks of the Aire, and not because she was by rights one day meant to hold the lands where the Aire rises and flows, which was a matter not to be spoken of. Husband Dorset was one of seven Tritones, sea demons.

Queen Anne the Dane was Tethys herself, Princess Elizabeth the Thames, while other ladies of the court played rivers of their connection, so that Lady Montgomery was the Severn, Lady Essex the Lea, Lady Arbella (Arabella) Stuart the Trent, and so on. Prince Henry was Oceanus but remained enthroned for the performance, being unwilling to disport, or embarrass, himself in the manner required. The masque began with a song that the rivers gave, so that the Titan Tethys could make her grand entrance. The words of the song ran thus:

Was ever hour brought more delight to mortal sight,
Than this, wherein fair Tethys deigns to show
Her and her nymphs arow
In glory bright?
See how we bring our flowers from out our wat'ry bowers,
To deck Apollo's tree,
The tree of Victory,
About whose verdant boughs
We pledge our happy vows,
And wish eternal Spring
To our glorious Ocean King.

In that summer of 1610, Lady Arbella Stuart was discovered to be married to William Seymour, duke of Somerset, who was thirteen years her junior and who, it was said, had been her lover as a boy. The match did not have the king's permission, unsurprisingly since it could have been seen as a bid for the throne. Arbella, great-granddaughter of Henry VII, was fourth in line and Seymour was sixth or thereabouts; cousin to them both was Lady Anne who had been very friendly with Arbella in their youth. Somerset was cast into the Tower and Lady Arbella imprisoned also, at a house in Lambeth. Like Lady Anne, Arbella had been cheated of her inheritance—she should have been countess of Lennox—but was denied Anne's freedom, and so lived a life largely of frustration and disappointment simply because of her birth.

Somerset was close to the throne through his descending from Henry VII's daughter and the brother of Henry VIII's third queen, Jane Seymour. These were thin lines of succession that King James did not want to be joined together to make thick. The marriage was a threat, a gathering place for those disaffected with the king's rule.

One day, this Somerset would become marquess of Hertford and a leading figure on the king's side in the dreadful wars to come. For the moment, his health was best served in the Tower. Lady Arbella would die in the Tower in 1615, after being captured at sea while trying to escape to France, driven into despair by her imprisonment, knowing that the king would never restore her to liberty. Her life was a lesson to those who would rise ever higher. Some said she was quite mad at the end and her dying at the age of forty was a blessed release for her. Had any of the schemes succeeded in putting her up for a queen, she would doubtless have lost the battle and her head. She was buried without ceremony in the tomb of Mary, Queen of Scots.

For Lady Anne, married life went on, divided between Knole and court, with the lord being mostly at court and the lady mostly at Knole, with no heavy sources of disagreement between the happy couple, although that was soon to change. In the meanwhile, there was another scandal at court.

Lady Anne's ex-suitor Sir Robert Kerr was made Viscount Rochester, set to go higher yet, being the king's favourite while also finding favour with one of the court's great beauties, the countess of Essex, Frances Howard. Frances had been married to the earl of Essex when he was aged thirteen and she fourteen, whereupon they were separated to prevent early pregnancy and, according to Lady Essex, had never consummated the marriage since. The lord of Essex claimed that he had no trouble in that connection with other women, but that his wife was so unpleasant to him that he could not bring himself to the act.

At about this time, Dorset told his wife of his intentions for travel in France and the Low Countries for some months. Lady Anne was not greatly enthusiastic about being left alone for what might be a year, but it was an engagement made before they were wed. After his next and much worse announcement, it seemed perhaps as well that he went abroad.

Dorset said he wished to seal the matter of his wife's inheritance by composing a settlement with her uncle of Cumberland. While acknowledging on all sides that her father's will was not as it should have been, Dorset argued that overturning it would prove impossible. The king had said that he would have things as they were, not as Lady Anne wished them, and the opinion of all the great lords and powers in the land were with the king.

Dorset continued that, Lady Anne's uncle being in the wrong but in possession, there should be a method whereby said uncle could be in the right, in conscience and *de facto*. This method, it was stated, should be a payment of monies. Uncle Cumberland had the Yorkshire lands for nothing, and wrongly, so if he had them for something, it would be rightly.

Lady Anne could see why her husband was proposing this. He lived generously. He gave to every cause, whether scholarly or in any other wise laudable. More to the case, he spent on his pleasures as if he disembarked every day from a ship that had been a year at sea. With more to spend, he would have sufficient he believed, whereas Lady Anne knew there could never be sufficient. A poor man with a few turnips on his plate could rightly think that a little meat would lead to sufficiency. A rich lord at court has a plate already full. To make it more, he would have the plate of gold, the knife of diamonds, the spoon of emeralds, and the dinner of unicorn's heart stuffed with phoenix eggs, which would sate him no better, would cost greatly, and lead only to quests for further glories.

Dorset's reasoning also concerned his wife's estates in their nature. He did not care for them. At Knole and at Bolebroke, his other house in Sussex, he could be lord of the hunt and whatever else, he could ride his horses and do what he willed, and a hundred souls were at his call to provide the best of everything. Then, whenever the fancy took him, he could soon be at whichever towns were holding races and fairs, and he could be at court, and he could stay there for courtly pleasures until they palled and country pleasures beckoned once more for a short while, then back to court.

Dorset had never been to Yorkshire nor Westmoreland, and he had no wish to go. Why, he would be not hours but days from court, and doubtless the northern country was full of hairy goblins, and nothing to eat but straw, porridge, and mutton fat, and nothing to drink but rainwater. There would be no one with any money to wager and nought to wager on but sheep, and for servants no more than a score of rough-tongued hunchbacks, crones, and doddards to look to his ease.

Genesis XXV xxxiii: And he sold his birthright unto Jacob.

Since he did not want Lady Anne's estates and had need of money, the answer was clearly to sell her birthright. Esau had very little for his birthright but a bowl of pottage, and Lady Anne should have had less. It would have been nothing for herself, for she should not have seen a farthing piece of any money Dorset might have persuaded out of her uncle, Cumberland, in his 'composition', as he called it, by which he meant the rearrangement of things into his notion of proper order.

In fact, Cumberland was quite willing to resolve matters in this way. In return for an *ex gratia* payment in cash, Lady Anne would give up all her claims in the north, Cumberland could live untroubled as a great man of Yorkshire and lands beyond, and the Dorsets would have some liquidity to maintain their courtly life.

Lady Anne said she would not agree, at which the earl grew angry and said that her obstinacy would lead to displeasure in the king. Further, she was disobeying her husband, when she had vowed to obey, which was against God's law, and she was going against the laws of nature in refusing to be led into the correct path by all the wise men of the realm, and she was going against the laws of England whose eye looked at the two, wife and husband, and saw only the husband. As she knew well enough, a wife's wealth was not her own to do with as she pleased. What would happen to the world if that were otherwise?

In his anger, he would vow never to see his wife again. He would go to France and, before his return, she should be installed with his grandmother in Great Dorset House in London. That this was mere hectoring and bluster did not make it any easier to bear. Lady Anne would pray to God that He helped her keep her resolve, for going against her husband, who was a good man otherwise, was chill to the soul.

It also showed a truly remarkable spirit. Everything was against Lady Anne. To be a woman wed to an earl may have given great rank and rich surroundings, but, in those who cared and looked beyond those trappings, it took away the sense of being a person. All of the woman's existence was absorbed into the husband's, so that, far from having any rights, the bride was no longer alive except as part of him. A wedded woman, in law if not always in practice, could not treat with another to buy a horse or have a joint-stool made, for she was not a legal body. She did not exist, except where woman's work was concerned—for instance in matters of dinner and dressing. If she agreed to purchase six pigs, it was a legal contract provided the pigs were to eat. If she agreed to purchase a new gown, likewise it was legal but the husband, if he did not like the gown, could sell it and his wife could not prevent him.

Since she had no wealth in money or property of her own, the wife could not be in debt and could not pursue a debtor. The husband had this responsibility, which made his wife his chattel. If Lady Anne had been plain Mistress Anne, Goodwife Anne, and not a countess with a certain station, she would have been no better in the law than the idiot who chattered in the village or the lunatic who howled in the asylum or the outlaw who roamed the woods. An ordinary wedded woman was indeed out of the law.

The law was made by men, administered by men, and changed by men when it suited them—there was no place in it for a woman. A woman had no place in anything except her household. She could not swear allegiance to the king yet had to hold that allegiance. She could hold any powerful office except queen of the realm, which position was available only to a small minority. She could be no parish constable nor lord mayor nor, God forbid, member of parliament. If she did inherit an ancient office, as Lady Anne did, and she became high constable of a hundred or sheriff of a county, she would likely have to give it up to her husband when she married or have it exercised by a surrogate, she being by nature, translated into law by men, less capable of logic, reason, and judgement than a man.

Had Lady Anne been born a male, she would have been 4th earl of Cumberland and a lawmaker in parliament. As one who felt aggrieved by the law, and who had the money to enlist the services of lawyers on her behalf, she would have to mind her reputation. Should she seek too strongly to right her wrongs, she would be talked of as one who makes a clatter, an inconsiderate malcontent who does not know her place on God's good earth.

At the other end of the scale from countesses and the like, there was a case of men's law in Penrith of a woman there who was a shrew to those who lived about her, forever complaining that such and such a thing was not to her liking and spreading tales of one to another that were false. Three men and three women went to the justice and denounced her as a scold, and the evidence was heard, and a fine was imposed of 2*s*. The woman had no money and could not pay, so the cucking stool was got out. She was made to take off her stockings and gather up her skirts and petticoats so that she was bare entirely below, and sat upon a chamber pot placed on the stool so that for all the world she was at the privy. With her hands tied behind her back and her feet tied together, the stool was hoisted aloft on to a kind of cart and pulled through the streets. People ran from their doors to see, and many a wise husband gave advice to his wife on the subject of scolding and what happened to those with long and loose tongues.

While Dorset was away in France and the Low Countries, Lady Anne's firm resolve prevailed. The matter was not brought up in the few letters he wrote, so she did as the felon and let the sleeping watchdog lie undisturbed. Her cousin, Margaret Clifford, daughter of Francis, 4th earl of Cumberland, sent news of her betrothal to Sir Thomas Wentworth, who was from Yorkshire and a lawyer, and eighteen years old. He was the son of Sir William of Wentworth Woodhouse, and great things were expected of him. Lady Margaret said he was quite the cleverest man she had met and the pride of the morning, which may or may not have been a good thing in a husband. Margaret would not live long enough to see Sir Thomas fulfil his promise, nor to see him end on the block.

> Proverbs XVI xviii: Pride goeth before destruction, and an haughty spirit before a fall.

If Lady Anne sometimes wondered at the many sided nature of her lord, how he could be a fine and loving husband one minute and a raging tyrant the next, she could take some comfort from the husband she so definitely rejected. Her suitor that was Sir Robert Kerr, who became the Viscount Rochester, who had been conducting a carnal dalliance with the lady of Essex, which was well known, had a close friend, Sir Thomas Overbury, a poet and man of letters. This Sir Thomas, who had known Robert Kerr since youthful days of obscurity, was greatly opposed to the dalliance and had said as much from the beginning.

In 1612, and it would be about February time, Sir Thomas went to war with the said countess, reviling her for a strumpet. He told Rochester that she did not warrant the title of whore, for a whore earned an honest penny with her work and did not cuckold her wedded husband in the public eye, and if Rochester ever did succeed in bringing such a vile and filthy woman to his lawful wife, it would be without any assistance from his oldest companion and to the ruin of his honour. Sir Thomas's loyalty was illustrated here, for many would have said that Lord Rochester's honour was not something to take a great deal of ruining.

Rochester went to his beloved and related Sir Thomas's every word, which threw her into a fury. Worse still, Sir Thomas wrote a lengthy poem that circulated the court and the streets of London in manuscript, called *The Wife*, which set forth the virtues of a wife as she should offer them and as an unmarried man should see them. Every person high and low in London knew what was meant by this and the lady of Essex who, before, did not mind who saw what she did, now cried out for justice, by which she meant that Sir Thomas should have a care.

> Jeremiah III vi: She is gone up upon every high mountain and under every green tree, and there hath played the harlot.
> 2 Kings IX xxx: And when Jehu was come to Jezreel, Jezebel heard of it; and she painted her face, and tired her head, and looked out at a window.

Whether Sir Thomas took precautions we do not know, but he had made a powerful enemy and a year later was thrown into the Tower. The talk was that the lord of Rochester had persuaded the king to offer Sir Thomas an embassy, that he would be the king's ambassador to the court of the new king of Russia, Tsar Michael Romanov. Then Rochester took Sir Thomas aside and convinced him against the position, who therefore gracefully declined it, following which Rochester went to the king and decried his old friend's refusal of the royal offer as an insult to the crown. Sir Thomas was charged with showing disrespect to King

James, which was enough to have him secured to await trial at the king's pleasure.

The Robert Kerr whom Lady Anne knew was not capable of such deceits. His mind could not have compassed a scheme with so many steps, much less conceived one. To find its originator, Sir Thomas might have looked to the sharper, more cunning and more contriving intelligence of the countess of Essex. She was about twenty-two years old, which sometimes showed in her indiscretion, but her brains had been born in her at the best quality.

Sir Thomas did not last long in the Tower and was found dead there. They said it was syphilis, the physicians, which it could have been. Some whispered that there were other gross kinds of dying most unwilling and painful, accompanied by sores and eruptions of the skin, which could be set in motion by a secret woman yet requiring no bodily meeting.

Hardly was Sir Thomas cold in his grave when Robert Kerr, Viscount Rochester, became the earl of Somerset and his paramour had petitioned the king for a nullity of her marriage to her husband, the noble if dull, wealthy if wearisome Robert Devereux, 3rd earl of Essex. It had been the king who pushed Essex into this ill match in the first place. Now the gay lady wished a second set of vows, on the grounds that her husband was feeble in the matter of fulfilling certain aspects of the marriage contract. If that were so, several lady courtiers could have testified that such an inhibition did not apply with them.

Luke XV xxiii: Bring hither the fatted calf, and kill it.

On 8 April 1612, Dorset was home from the Low Countries. He would have been welcomed in great strength by the household and by Lady Anne herself, who would have hoped that love would conquer all. The usual thing was to gather what they could of spring flowers and herbs, such as rosemary, young walnut leaves, thyme, and apple blossom, and, with dried lavender and rose petals from store, perfume the bedchamber with sweet odours. Alas, its powers were insufficient.

Doubtless spurred on by his brother Edward's talk, who had taken up the position of 'enemy' *versus* Lady Anne, and who she believed could not be trusted with a penny piece for the church poor box, Dorset once more rehearsed his arguments, by which Cumberland would pay money *ex gratia* to assuage his guilt and, by accepting it, Lady Anne would acknowledge his right to her inheritance.

Lady Anne's stratagem was, as before, one of silent disagreement. As a sheep will shelter behind a bush until the storm passes over its head, so she sheltered and waited patiently for the thunder and lightning to pass over, which it did. Dorset could not understand her obduracy on this subject, and asked why she made such a commotion over a few acres of moorland and a few broken castles that nobody of quality could possibly want. Her reply was silence, noting to herself that any commotion was not of her making.

News came to Knole that another great funeral was due, Lord Cecil, earl of Salisbury, having died and with him had gone a great deal of wisdom. By his tireless efforts as lord treasurer and the king's chief minister, he had much saved the king against his natural profligacy although not entirely, that being a task beyond any mortal, and he would be dearly missed. It was he who secured King James's succession when he served Queen Elizabeth. Now about the court there in 1612, those who would advise the king were mostly light and fancy fellows, without the steady hand and eye of Salisbury. The king and queen together, without their rock and stay, would surely overrun their purses in a moment.

Salisbury had the name Wryneck and Crookback, and Queen Elizabeth called him her Pygmy, but his mind in commerce could bring in money to match that which went out. A royal palace without filled coffers was a most unsteady place, and it took no time after the news of Salisbury's death was abroad for the London brewers to refuse to supply the royal household, being without payment and now not likely to get any.

More sorrowful news came in November. The Prince of Wales was dead of a fever at eighteen years. The lord of Dorset had lost a companion of his heart and a true friend, and he felt the cut deeper than most.

Prince Henry had been a good figure of a man, of reddish hair and much admired with, many said, the abilities of his Tudor forebear Henry VIII. As he also inherited the strengths and attractive qualities of his father and mother without the lesser aspects thereof, surely he would have become a truly excellent king. The country was left with the younger brother, Charles, duke of York, who was very small and quiet by comparison with the late prince, and physically feeble. As a child, he had been unable to walk without special iron boots, and the general opinion was that he would not last long enough to marry and produce heirs to the Stuart line. His sister, Elizabeth, aged sixteen, was soon to marry Frederick V, Elector Palatine, which raised the possibility of a German successor to the thrones of England and Scotland. King James would have much to do in education if his second son was to find the kingly qualities in himself that everyone saw so abundantly in Henry.

The funeral was of the greatest magnificence, as if for a king, and at once rumours spread through court and town that Prince Henry died not of a fever given by God but of one delivered to him in a drinking cup. The prince was a staunch opponent of the old religion, though his mother was a follower of it, and some said that the Catholics and their sympathisers feared persecution should he come to the throne. Of these scandalmongers, a few were such bigots as to say that his own mother had had a hand in his death, which was beyond any credence. These were the foulest lies and were put about by Puritans and others who would have had all Catholics burned at the stake, buried in lime, flayed alive, or drawn and quartered, being their final solution or purgative for washing the old religion away.

Less heralded but more immediately painful was news of the death of Lady Frances Bourchier, daughter of the earl of Bath and Elizabeth Russell, sister to Lady Anne's mother. Lady Frances and Lady Anne had been childhood friends and confidantes in adulthood, and at this time, when beset by men who would disinherit her, Anne needed friends more than ever.

In February 1613, the marriage of Princess Elizabeth and Frederick, Count Palatinate of Heidelburg, called the Elector Frederick V, was celebrated in such style as the world had never seen, with feasts and revels enough to tire Bacchus. Some of the older courtiers called it excessive, disorderly, rough, and overloud. The younger ones replied that if you were going to watch a battle on the Thames between Turks and Venetians, would you have it quiet and well mannered?

Never was more money spent at a wedding by a man who was neither the bridegroom nor the bride's father. Dorset was so keen for outshining everyone else in his lavishings on the king's daughter that gold became raindrops in his hands. Every part of the festival felt his generosity. Master Shakespeare, though said to be in country retirement, at the lord's commission composed a wedding masque to be fitted into a performance of his play called *The Tempest*, which was done at court with miraculous tricks of magic, and everything in it paid for by the purse of Dorset. Doubtless he wished to show the world how princely his virtues were and be praised for it, but he was generous by his nature and open hearted. His virtues, alas, did not include that ability to spend only the money he had.

Everyone at court marvelled at his bountiful bestowals and largesses, applauded the play to the rafters, and made of him a hero of his time, while Lady Anne smiled graciously and waited for the storm after the calm.

Luke XVI xxviii: For which of you, intending to build a tower, sitteth not down first, and counteth the cost, whether he have sufficient to finish it?

After that, little above the ordinary was happening at court and the earl seemed to have forgotten or put aside for the moment his composition for Lady Anne's estates. When the Globe theatre burned down, there was much talk of rival companies setting it on fire but no solid thing came of that, and then the news was all of water, being the opening of the New River in September, which was finished at the Round Pond by the village of Islington. All the court attended the ceremony; though it was still the plague season, there could hardly be any plague at Islington where there was nothing but fields, cows, and dairy maids.

This New River was an idea begun in the time of Queen Elizabeth, the city authorities having signally failed to persuade the populace that running water and ordure were best kept apart. Still the common people threw their waste wherever they pleased, and the answer seemed to be to bring in water from outside the city where it had not been contaminated. There were springs in Hertfordshire, and those waters could be gathered together and run in a new river course to be built by men.

There were objections. Some said that men should not make rivers, it being the work of God. Some said it was an impossible feat, but a plan was shown to the queen requiring engineering work of the greatest precision, for a river 40 miles long, twisting and turning to maintain a gentle decline so that no intervention was needed for the water to flow, and this would be a drop of less than 6 inches a mile. The work faltered many times and saw many new masters, but the river was rescued and pressed by the king who saw great benefits in it, and so it was completed and fresh water flowed for those many who had not their own wells.

In August 1613, Lady Anne's brother-in-law, Edward Sackville, who was no friend, was challenged to a duel by his friend, the young Lord Bruce of Kinloss, possibly over a complex matter involving a lady, Venetia Stanley, a society beauty, or another. The duel took place in the Netherlands; Sackville received severe wounds from which he eventually recovered, but Lord Kinloss was killed aged nineteen. Venetia maintained a close connection with the Sackvilles, most especially with Lady Anne's husband, Richard.

By November, Lady Anne was fairly confident she was with child but decided not to tell the earl until after Christmas, when she would be sure. In the meanwhile, she had to avoid all upsets and pray that the earl did not berate her more about her ancient lands, for that gave her boiling senses fit to burst.

> Ecclesiasticus VIL i: Let us now praise famous men, and our fathers that begat us.

And so the year turned, and the earl was full of joys at the news and most solicitous for his wife's health. He consulted every fount of wisdom and prescribed all manner of elements in a regimen to assure her of safe carriage. While collecting knowledge from every source, he remained in the idea that his was the first wife ever to bear a child and he the first husband to father one.

As if this were not enough, Lady Anne was enjoined on all sides to restrict her imagination to wholesome matters lest her thoughts injure the child. She must eat plain food, lest she corrupt the natural inclinations of her child with her gluttony. No sin could be committed, in thought, word, or deed for, in the committing, the sinner might add to the original burden of her child's soul or give him a deformity of the body.

Indeed, where a child was misshapen, the degree of monstrosity was matched with the degree of the mother's sins. Wiseacres might say that they had seen perfection in the child of lady 'X', while it was likely that the father was not her husband, and moreover that her sins during its carrying warranted a twisted leg at the least.

Then, it was the duty of Master Dupper, the Knole chaplain, to sermonise Lady Anne and to ask all the household to pray for the forgiveness of her sins so that the pain and injury of the birth should be no more than necessary. Such pain was to atone for the sin of Eve in the Garden but, with prayer, extra punishments from God might be avoided. The old Greek poet Euripides and our English poet Master Shakespeare agreed that the sins of the father shall be visited upon the son. These must be sins visited through the seed of the father, therefore sins committed after conception could not matter in this connection.

Lady Anne's own sins were not so carefree, for they could seep from her soul to the child's by way of her blood through all the nine months of carrying, which was yet another imbalance between husband and wife. If a pregnant woman saw a hare running across her path, that might be the cause of the child having a hare lip. Her husband, if he so wished, could hunt and course hares all day and every day with no such lip being a possibility.

In June 1614, the place of confinement was prepared at Great Dorset House in London and the room darkened, and Lady Anne's cousins and friends invited to attend close to or nearby. Many enquiries had been made regarding midwives and her choice, Mistress Gough, was well spoken of everywhere. There was some gossip that the earl would not allow her, she having attended that certain lady 'X' aforesaid, nor was he entirely sanguine over the matter of Mistress Gough's fee, which was to be £40. This compared rather unfavourably with the last midwife to attend at Knole, which was for one of the servant women, who had made a charge of 5*s* 4*d*, and that had been put high for mother being in the service of an earl. Mistress Gough had charged £32 when attending lady 'X', in which case, if lady 'X' was worth £32, the countess of Dorset was worth £320.

There was also the subject of milk feeding. Lady Anne would rather her child was at her own breast than a nurse's, and the earl agreed. Some husbands less gentle than he would have had the child off to a wet-nurse as soon as could be, that the wife's milk might dry up and the conception of further children be under business sooner. Some husbands less gentle still would take their wives, as their right, without allowance for any healing time, whether or not this might cause pain again to the wife and, say the physicians, despoil the milk. The earl did not seem unduly dismayed by the prospect of a wifeless bed to share with himself for some months.

The dowager countess of Cumberland came down from the north in readiness, which was a great comfort, for no woman giving birth to her first child can be without fears for herself. Pain is certain, much pain, and the child was great within her and she would be rid of it, for the relief of the burden and to earn some respite from physicians and from every one of the household who had ever had anything to do with a child being born. If there was one thing for the child that must certainly be done above all else, there were a thousand such.

So, Lady Anne was placed in the hands of Mistress Gough to do what she told her, and if that should go awry, it should be the will of God and no other. Death of itself did not hold fears, for Lady Anne felt safe in the Lord her God, but regrets would be many to leave a husband and a life behind with so much undone. Illness was more greatly feared, but women of the Clifford strain and of her mother's Russell family had always proved strong bearers of their husband's children, and there was no reason that Anne Clifford should prove an exception to the rule.

Proverbs XVIII x: The name of the Lord is a strong tower: the righteous runneth into it, and is safe.

On 2 July, the child was born, a girl lusty and hale, to be called Margaret after her grandmother. Dorset would have had a son, as would all with heirdoms to pass, but he was pleased that his daughter was well, that his wife was well, that the birth was well, and that they had made a little Sackville between them. At the least, it showed that such things could be done.

Lady Anne's mother contrived to miss the birth, having come all the way from Westmoreland for it. On the day, she was sure that her daughter's labours were not yet come to a nicety and so decided to make further investigations into the ancient laws of inheritance. She went to meet some learned gentlemen at the library, kept in the Tower, of laws, attestations, and rolls of court, there to blow the dust from papers made by King William the Conqueror, King Alfred the Great, King Caractacus, the Emperor Claudius, and, for all anyone knew, the Green Man of the Forest. The proof of the inheritances was already established. No more proof was needed nor could be found. What was required was a persuasion of the king that their case was right and just. More ancient records could do nothing in that cause, but Lady Margaret lived in hope and became so engrossed that she missed the locking of the Tower gates, had to stay the night there, and was absented from the birth.

On the following day, there was the christening, and here Lady Margaret made the vows of godmother to the child named for her, the new Lady Margaret, but straightway made preparations for her leave taking. She wished to journey back to Brougham without delay and therefore they brought forward the churching. As with the christening, the Reverend Doctor Valentine Carey, dean of St Paul's, came to them and they said their prayers, which were of thanksgiving after childbirth.

Mistress Gough had warned Lady Anne severely that it would be ill luck to go abroad from the house until she was churched, which was the only part of the midwife's services where a fault could be found. In the old religion, this rite was called the purification of women, and Leviticus has it that women are unclean after birth and perhaps such bad luck is tangled up with this notion of uncleanness. In the modern church of 1614, the interpretation was one of thanksgiving, and someone of Lady Anne's mind would have given that hearty endorsement, for she was thankful to the bottom of her heart but in no way did she feel unclean.

8

Persecution and Defiance

The news from court in the late summer of 1614 was that Lady Anne's old suitor, Robert Kerr, duke of Somerset, was displaced in the king's affections by a Ganymede, a cup bearer of such grace and handsomeness that Jove himself wept with envy and wished him brought to the dining halls of the gods. This peerless beauty was George Villiers, son of old Sir George, squire of Brooksby, and many were the whispering lips at the king's ear, pressing the case of Villiers against Somerset, which was largely to bring about the fall of the duke rather than the rise of young George or anybody else.

Such are the vanities and idiocies of courtiers that they watch and encourage the rise of one, then believe that his disgrace and the rise of another will prove a benefit, and all turning on the accidental arrangement of a face. If quality and beauty went together in reliable fashion, life would be simple indeed, if unfortunate for some.

That the king did prefer his new Ganymede was widely acknowledged, he having likened this same to Saint Stephen and nicknamed him Steenie for it. Little time went by before Villiers was made gentleman of the bedchamber, then master of the horse, and his star shone ever more brilliantly.

> Acts VI xv: And all that sat in the council, looking steadfastly on him, saw his face as it had been the face of an angel.
>
> Matthew XXIII xxvii: Ye are like unto whited sepulchres, which indeed appear beautiful outward, but are within full of dead men's bones and of all uncleanness.

Letters were exchanged between dowager and countess, and gifts sent for the new Lady Margaret such as a pair of delicate fine little gloves. Lady Anne hoped to journey north before the winter set in but 'my Lord will not by any means give his consent that I should go, till the business between my uncle of Cumberland and him be ended.' Meanwhile, Lady Anne kept careful watch in case an arrangement should be made, with Cumberland's son, Henry, and Dorset's brother, Edward, all cunning against her, conspiring and blowing on the coals. Regardless of what the men might decide among themselves, they could do nothing without Lady Anne's agreement, and that they should not have at any price.

In any case, such arrangements had to be suspended while the professors of law took their turn. Lady Anne's mother had entered a suit to have her husband's will declared invalid, on those grounds already well-rehearsed, and expected the upshot to be as an apple pip planted in the garden. Should we wish to discover it before it sprouts, it cannot be found, and we must wait many a long season for it to bear fruit if it grows at all. There were few, or no, hopes of the lawyers. The case was clear, but such clarity had had no reward thus far, and so mother and daughter did not look to the sword of justice to smite the Philistines on their behalf.

Those men of the law who would have had the ladies believe they wielded this sword with no partiality or favour would cogitate and ponder, weigh in the balances, argue the finest points among themselves, stroke their beards if they had them or scratch their noses if they had not, weigh in the balances again, ponder three times more, and cogitate a fourfold. When all was done, they would come to Lady Margaret and say 'this is a matter we cannot resolve. By the by, we should be most grateful if our account, equating in proximity to a prince's ransom, could be settled forthwith in good English money, and we thank you, your Ladyship.'

As the winter wore on, little Margaret grew apace and, said Lady Anne, looked each day more like her father, which Dorset denied saying that his daughter and his wife were one person in the glass. The earl was contented with his daughter, although, like all men, he saw her only when nothing else pressed. Bringing children into the world, and furnishing them for the world, was and—so the men believed—always would be the trade of women. Fathers such as the earl may well have shown no interest in a son until the age of seven, when he was deemed suitable for breeches, his child's clothes could be put away and he may be transported from the nursery to the company of boys and men. For the daughter, some fathers may never have shown any interest at all until the question of her marriage arose.

Daughter or son, their children had much to be thankful for. Were one a child of a poor family, it could be taken by the worthy rulers of the parish and placed to an apprenticeship, to learn to be a housemaid or a pantryman, and if it did not learn it to the satisfaction of master or mistress, it would be beaten, and all this from seven years old. Cliffords and Sackvilles had no such concerns. Little Margaret would have the best of everything, but she would not be allowed to see only this side of life. Her mother would teach her the hard parts of the world so she would know that there, but for the grace of God, she went.

She would learn to read first, that she could have the bible from the earliest time, and to write and to figure. When little Meg was seven years, she would be a learned gentlewoman, not an apprentice to a slave captain in drudgery, yet she should have a childhood, for those poor girls of the parish are sent forth to earn their keep as soon as might be. Folk did not expect a foal to do the work of a mare, but such was expected of the children of the common people.

Little Meg would likewise learn the virtues, and those especial to women, which are chastity, obedience, and modesty, yet she was a Clifford in bloodline and Lady Anne's daughter, which was to hope that she would preserve her mind for herself and not be led by fools and those who would use her for their gain.

The thin days of May passed, when there seemed to be nothing to eat but eggs and salt fish, and June 1615 held forth the promise of summer's plenty. Little Meg was almost a year old and could crawl half the length of the Long Gallery at Knole, which was about the longest gallery in England, and she was like to be running the whole of it shortly. The proud mother watched and smiled her pride, and all seemed peace and light. That a black cloud hovered, ready to cover the sun, could be forgotten for days at a time, only to return.

Dorset came to Lady Anne one day in a fearful rage, saying that it was common gossip about the court that the king was selling titles to pay his debts. Lady Anne said this was old news, for he had been selling baronetcies at £1,000 for a good while. But no, cried Dorset, much worse. The king had been offering earldoms for sale at £10,000. Why, here was he, an earl by birth and right and, he hoped, to become the father of another earl in waiting, but without £10,000 to spare, while any self-seeking charlatan who had acquired such a sum, by whatever means, could exchange it for an ermine gown and the trappings of nobility, and have himself called lord and his wife, whatever kind of a whore she might have been, called countess.

Such a lack of ready money soon transferred his thoughts to the inheritance and the accommodation he so earnestly wished. He forbade her to stir beyond the grounds of Knole, saying that matters must be resolved between himself and Cumberland before she could do any such thing. There was no profit in Lady Anne pointing out that if any matters were to be resolved, they would be between Cumberland and herself, not Cumberland and Dorset.

The earl had great debts, this she knew, and was much bowed down and compressed in spirit. He loved her as ever, and she him, but he saw her constancy over the inheritance as the bar to his escape from his obligations. If she were to agree to this composition with Cumberland, he, her husband, would be as new, he believed.

He also believed he had the law newly on his side, since the first action in the trial of Lady Margaret's petition—that her late husband's will had been illegal—had been heard in the Court of Common Pleas. This medieval court, established by Magna Carta, heard disputes between citizen and citizen, which therefore did not directly concern the king. Any conflicts over land and property generally ended up here, at Westminster. Uncle Cumberland, son, Edward, and the earl of Dorset had all agreed to be bound by the decision of the four judges sitting. Unsurprisingly, said judges found against Lady Margaret, but Lady Anne would have nothing to do with it and refused to accept the judgement.

A small number of persons thought Lady Anne in the right. Almost everybody in the world thought she was wrong and should put her duty to her husband above all else, but what then of her mother? Lady Margaret had worked without rest ever since her husband died to restore the inheritance to her daughter and to restore the estates in Westmoreland to good repair. Was daughter to throw all this in her mother's face? Was she to shoot an arrow into her mother's heart, to pay the debts of a profligate husband? Such an act would never be considered and her knowledge of her husband made her doubly adamant. Never in all their contentions over this subject had Dorset made promise that, with his debts paid, he would live more modestly. He had never mentioned such a possibility. Doubtless he would continue in his old ways, spending money he did not have nor would have in the sure and certain hope that someone would find the pot of gold at the end of the rainbow with 'Property of the Earl of Dorset' written on it.

All storms blow over, for a while anyway, and forgetful days of summer joined themselves into weeks when, with a tumult and uproar, certain news flew along the highways and every byway with the speed of a musket ball. The talk was so great and by so many that it would have drowned a battle's noise. Old murmurings and whispers had grown into cries aloud, that Sir Thomas Overbury died not of disease but of poison. How the word escaped so long after his death was not described, but there had been a conspiracy, and so it could be thought that one of those conspirators had been unable to stand the guilt any longer.

No lesser inquisitors than Sir Edward Coke, chief justice of the King's Bench, and Sir Francis Bacon, the attorney general, were set to unravel the strands of mystery, which implied that the king saw guilt in those close to himself. It was put about that the lady of Somerset, late of Essex, had had the most to gain from Sir Thomas's demise or, if vengeance were not entirely the province of the good Lord above, the most reason to want him dead, he being her enemy in the matter of her lover and second husband. Lady Somerset, being a Howard, was a first cousin to Dorset. Her father and his mother were brother and sister, and so the links were too close for comfort.

If it was she, then it followed that the earl of Somerset, Robert Kerr, Lady Anne's suitor-that-would-have-been, must likewise have been a weaver of the fabric of the plot, and there must have been agents too, for the lord and lady could hardly go to the Tower themselves to dose poor Sir Thomas there in his confinement. Now that Somerset was no longer the golden god that he once had been, after displacement from the king's favour by the more glorious shining light of wonder that was Master Villiers, it was uncertain that the king's protection would be much extended, unless Somerset had some dark secrets of the king that could not be let out.

So many great names were mentioned in one breath of the Overbury business that it scarce could be believed that it took them all to ensure the death of one man. The Tower's lieutenant, a chief officer of the king, was accused, which entangled more of the Howard family since the old Lord Chamberlain, father of Lady Somerset, had had this lieutenant appointed. The lord privy seal of the time, an uncle, was connected also but he had recently taken the precaution of dying and so could not answer for himself.

So, the lieutenant of the Tower, Sir Gervase Helwys, was hanged on Tower Hill for being complicit in the murder and the hounds were loose, baying every secret to the sky. All was revealed, or almost all. The lady of Somerset confessed to murder and was held at a secure house, while her husband cried his innocence. Soon dead by common hanging were their friends in this matter, being the widow of a physician, Mistress Turner; Sir Thomas's jailer, Master Weston; and an apothecary, Master Franklin, who supplied rosalger and copper vitriol though he had said he did not know the purpose. With Somerset's gold to persuade past any reluctance, these three had been well qualified for their task and thus had their reward. Whether their captains would follow into the noose was another question, though they were promised it by the talk of the town. As if to make pause in the proceedings, in December 1615, Lady Somerset was delivered of a child, a daughter, who was Lady Anne Kerr.

On New Year's Day 1616, our Lady Anne stayed in her chamber with two friends to supper, Frances Wray, second wife of Sir Robert Rich, later earl of Warwick, and 'my sister Sackville,' Mary Curzon, wife of Sir Edward Sackville, later to become governess of the children of King Charles. Dorset and all his company went to the masque at court, presented before the king and queen, which Lady Anne did go to see on twelfth night. This was a Ben Jonson production, called *Christmas, His Show*, meant to promote the traditional keeping of the Christmas festival against the hostile attitude of the Puritans.

Two days later, Lady Anne went to visit Lady Ralegh in the Tower, where she had been imprisoned with Sir Walter since 1603. Sir Walter's alleged treason was soon to be forgotten when he was sent to South America to find El Dorado, a doomed mission if ever there was one. Lady Ralegh, Bess Throckmorton that was and a cousin of Catherine Parr (Henry VIII's sixth), had been a gentlewoman of the Privy Chamber to Queen Elizabeth. The latter had been most displeased when she discovered that her gentlewoman had become pregnant by her favourite rascal Walter Ralegh and, even worse, married him without the queen's consent. A short stay in the Tower ensued, where Bess later would spend more of her married life than at Sherborne, the Ralegh estate.

The 14th was a pleasant day, with Lady Anne losing £15 at gleek (or glecko) to two of her friends and having a merry supper with two more, Dorset being elsewhere. It was to be the last time of any kind of joy for some long while. Next day, Lady Anne had two sets of company, both with the same message. Supper guest from the night before Lady Frances Grantham gave it kindly and with love in her heart, but it coincided exactly with that brought by Lady Anne's cousin, Russell, earl of Bedford, he being nephew to Lady Anne's dear mother who had been Margaret Russell. He set to and berated poor Anne, shouting and bellowing and bawling, and her every fault he cried out clamorously and listed her errors as if he were Moses reading the Ten Commandments to Satan. He meant it for the best and had no thought to be cruel, but Lady Anne could not bear it and she wept while he was there and long after he had gone.

It grieved her sorely that all those whom she would love, and who would love her, were set to fight her except for a very few. She was doing nought but what was her right, to keep her own to her, but the world and his wife would have had her throw her worth in the river. How she prayed to the good Lord to keep her strong of purpose, for at every turn there were armies of angels and devils together, who would have made her cry surrender.

For recreation to her spirit she met her cousin, Lady Wotton, at court, and they took a few turns around Whitehall, then Lady Anne went to the Abbey at Westminster, there to walk about the tombs and think of those whose plight had been worse than her own, such as Queen Mary of Scots. Lady Anne walked for an hour there and studied the inscriptions, and came home to Great Dorset House via the river, where she was much chilled and felt worse than when she had set forth. Her feelings were made double by remembrance of what must happen on the morrow.

The morrow came, and what a collection was there at Great Dorset House, all of a mind. How much better it would have been to have kept to her chamber with black mustard, willow bark, and wintergreen for her cold, but she could not. The archbishop of Canterbury took her to himself for above an hour, during which he persuaded and chided and told her all that she had heard before so many times, that she must set her hand to the new draftings of the lawyers, which he said was the will of God, which was to reject her mother's suit that her father's will be nullified, and therefore to give away her inheritance of her ancient lands in return for monies paid to her husband.

Lady Anne listened to this archbishop, George Abbot, who owed his preferment to the Sackvilles, in particular the present earl's grandfather. The Abbot family had been mercers in Guildford; George had had a scholarship to Balliol and, with Sir Thomas Sackville's help, had risen to vice-chancellor of Oxford. His was one of the great minds responsible for the new Bible. He had been the king's intermediary during the king's efforts to take bishops to Scotland, and he had been royally advanced all the way to primate of England. Since it was a Sackville who wanted Lady Anne's inheritance renounced, and the king wanted the same, the archbishop was twice placed to act the diplomat without favour.

Lady Anne might have pointed out that her birthright consisted of six castles, that part of Yorkshire called Craven, and a large portion of land in Westmoreland, whereas his birthright consisted of a house and a few bales of cloth in Guildford. Even so, regardless of the disparity, would the archbishop like to sell his birthright for money to be used in feasting and wagering on cockfights? Because that was what she was being asked to do.

After an hour and a half, the archbishop conceded defeat in his solo mission and ushered Lady Anne into the gallery where awaited her inquisitors and adversaries together, but not including her husband. There was Lord William Howard, Dorset's uncle against whom her mother had warned her; cousin, Bedford; Lady Anne's chief tormentor, Dorset's brother, Edward Sackville; the 16th baron de Ros; and 'a great company of men of note'.

Lady Anne had rehearsed her answer but kept it until they had finished flattering her and terrifying her by turns, prevailing and pleading, smiling and frowning, praising and vexing, bullying and fawning, beguiling and making menace, until she thought she must be pulled apart in pieces or pushed down into her own shoes and through the floor.

She was offered pen and ink, and great documents were presented, and she should set her hand to them, and at last she gave her reply, which was that she would not set her hand to anything until she had consulted with her dear mother, as the whole matter concerned Lady Margaret's jointure as well as the inheritance and, indeed, the lawsuit was hers.

This the assembled lords saw as a weakening of her resolve. They believed that their persuasions had had some effect for she was not saying no outright. Lady Anne saw it as a way of gaining time and a way of being free for a while of such great forces, for surely never before had such a gathering of the mighty been held over so small a matter as a woman's wish.

In any case, did this matter not go deeper than lands and castles alone? Did all these men of note care so much that Dorset's purse was filled? Or was there a principle here, an original opinion which they sought to set as a law of nature and God—that a woman should not stand against a man in a matter of property? When Lady Anne defied her husband and the all the powers in the land, she was shaking the foundation stone of the confederacy of men that was England. She was blowing a trumpet before the walls of Jericho, and liable to make them fall flat again.

In answer to her answer, the assembled lords, as if they were a properly constituted court, were glad to set a limitation of 22 March, by which time the countess of Dorset should have journeyed north to her mother, consulted therewith, and returned with all good will to put signature to their papers. Or no. There had to be the possibility of no, but the lords did not give much weight to it. They were certain of their victory, and it was they and not Lady Anne who dipped pens in ink and put their names to documents, setting forth these conditions.

This was a day the world could not credit. All had believed that by the end of it, Lady Anne should either be disinherited under seal of agreement, or else become a wife in waiting of divorce. She was neither of these. For a time, she could be merry and her husband could be kind to her, and she could send word to all the ladies of her acquaintance that she was set for the north.

Dorset announced his intentions of escorting his wife northwards, and they would go in two coaches with four horses apiece. Lady Anne would be attended by Mistress Willoughby and one of the Mistresses Simpton, Judith. The earl would have only one man with him and the rest would be horsemen. They were to leave on 21 February 1616, and by another way than her last journey, which this time would take them to Dunstable, Stony Stratford, Towcester, Warwick, and Lichfield, then to Derby, on an old road though not much used and not much populated with good houses. Worse, beyond Derby, to Manchester, there lay the most dangerous moors and mountains in England where coaches never went.

Lady Anne hoped to be glad of her lord's company, though when they arrived at Brougham, he would be sure to expect her to persuade her mother to agree with his composition, which would cause angry discord between two of the three people whom she loved most in the world. Her daughter, Margaret, was too young yet to adventure such a way.

The way to Lichfield seemed very, very long. The earl and countess lay together at an inn at Dunstable and then likewise at Towcester and Warwick, where they saw the castle, and thence to stay at an inn at Lichfield for two nights. Sunday 25 February was their wedding anniversary. They went twice to church, to the famous cathedral of three spires, and the next day they would take the old straight road to Derby, where they had lodgings spoken for at an inn. At the least, so was the intent.

The bishop of Lichfield came to see them at the inn and they broke their fast together, talking of light matters when, of a sudden, the story goes that the earl asked the bishop his opinion on the composition proposed with Cumberland. The bishop feigned not to know the ins and outs and would have expressed no opinion at all, yet Dorset did launch himself into a volley of hot speech in which he set forth his argument and denounced Lady Anne for a stubborn intractable, an obstinate vixen, and an unmoveable tree stump.

The bishop protested in a meek and mild way that it was little to do with him, and he looked with anxiety at the said tree stump that was weeping freely, but Dorset would have none of it and demanded his episcopal view. Still the bishop, to his great credit, demurred in his place and the earl stamped his feet and strode away out of the room in a fury. The good bishop bade Lady Anne dry her eyes and sent for his men to help their own to prepare the coaches and horses in the inn yard.

Lady Anne and her two women boarded their coach at the appointed time and waited a good half an hour before Dorset appeared and got into his coach without look or word. He made signal to Lady Anne's man Rivers, who was driving, to set away first and lead the procession, and thus they made their unhappy way. They called at Croxall Hall, ancient seat of the Curzons (which, by marriage in 1622, would come into the Sackville estate), and on to Burton-on-Trent where one of his lordship's men rode up and bade Rivers stop the coach as he had a message for the countess, which he gave her, it being short and clear. The lord of Dorset had decided to attend some races at Lichfield instead of going to Westmoreland.

Lady Anne could have got down from her coach and looked back along the road, to see the other going away with more than half their company of men and horses. She would have said to the messenger to convey her thanks to Lord Dorset and to wish him good health and God's speed. Then she climbed back into her coach and was miserable all to Derby.

In the morning, a man was sent ahead to Hardwick, for the proposal had been to see the earl of Devonshire's two houses there, the newer one built next to the old by the former countess of Shrewsbury, remembered in Lady Anne's young days at court as a terrible and powerful old woman called Bess of Hardwick, who was grandmother to Arbella Stuart. The second Hardwick Hall had been intended as the home of the future Queen Arbella of England, but they had King James instead. Bess began another great house called Chatsworth, hard by Baslow in this same county of Derbyshire, and this was hardly off their route by much but they did not go to it.

After Hardwick, they pressed on to Chesterfield and lay at an inn, and to Rotherham likewise, and thence by very bad roads to Penistone, where there was no inn so Lady Anne lodged with the poor parson there. She might have been almost glad now that the earl was not with her for he would have found in the parson's house much to complain of, while the parson could do no more than his best.

Roger de Clifford married into the de Viteripont (Vieuxpont) family *c.* 1270 and with his bride, Isabella, came considerable estates in Westmoreland and Cumberland, including castles at Brougham, Appleby, Brough, and Mallerstang. The latter was known as Pendragon and supposedly belonged to Uther Pendragon, father of King Arthur, but no one has been able to find any evidence for this.

The Normans put it up in the early twelfth century, and by 1170, it was in the hands of Sir Hugh de Morville, who had the title lord of Westmoreland and was one of the quartet of knights who murdered St Thomas à Becket in 1170.

The Scots attacked Mallerstang/Pendragon several times, leaving it a ruin by 1541, and thus it remained until Lady Anne came along in 1649. She was single-minded about her castles. A rational, disinterested survey of her inheritance would have concluded that a residence in Yorkshire (Skipton) and one in Westmoreland (Appleby) were enough for good management of the estates, but Lady Anne would have all her castles put to rights.

Coming after Lady Anne and her enthusiasm, her sons-in-law and their successors could see no use for Mallerstang castle and so robbed it of anything moveable, including the lead from the roof. By the 1770s, much had collapsed, and the photograph shows the building as it is now (October 2018).

Lady Anne's mother, Margaret Russell, the youngest of seven children, was born in 1560 and grew up with an aunt, Alice, Lady Elmes, at Lilford Hall in Northamptonshire. Margaret went back to the family seat, Chenies Manor, on the Buckinghamshire–Hertfordshire border, aged about nine, where a sister and two of her brothers were still living, along with a husband-to-be. The law of magnetism states that unlike poles attract, which seems to have been borne out by the teenagers Margaret Russell and George Clifford, who were described by Lady Anne: 'She was pensive and delicate, he adventurous and fond of display. Her spirit never yielded to ill fortune or opposition', which characteristics would be much needed in one married to a young man whose own personality led him simultaneously into national hero status and crippling debt.

Lady Anne's father, George Clifford, was born in 1558 at Brougham castle in Westmoreland. Her grandfather, Henry, 2nd earl of Cumberland and 12th baron de Clifford, died when George was eleven, in 1569, making him 13th baron and 3rd earl. He became a national hero, Queen Elizabeth's champion, and died in October 1608 as the Rt Hon. earl of Cumberland, knight of the garter, Baron Clifford, baron and sheriff of Westmoreland, lord of the honour of Skipton, etc. This portrait of him is a reworking of a Nicholas Hilliard miniature, done in 1588 when he was thirty but repainted at a 'normal' size after his death.

Above: This picture shows the parents with the two Clifford boys. The first child, Francis, was born in 1584; the second, Robert, in 1585. Francis died in 1589 with his mother carrying a baby due in two months. Robert was sickly and his father was hoping very much for another boy, but in January 1590, a girl was born at Skipton castle, to be christened Anne. The second heir, Robert, died like his brother aged five years and eight months, in 1591.

Opposite above: Brougham castle, as it is now, birthplace of George Clifford, was the favourite home in later years of Lady Anne's mother, Lady Margaret, and of Lady Anne herself. Both noble ladies died there.

Opposite below: Henry Clifford, known as The Shepherd Lord, followed the country life. He went up to London and the Court only when called to take his seat in parliament, otherwise spending his time at Barden Tower, that had been a hunting lodge for Skipton castle but which he remodelled into a comfortable residence with an observatory, for he developed a great interest in astronomy and its then sister science, astrology. Lady Anne restored it, but the interest was not maintained.

Lady Anne, here at about the age of fifteen, was a favourite at the court of Queen Elizabeth, but her hopes of high preferment were dashed when the queen died. Lady Anne was deemed not tall enough to walk in the funeral procession.

The young Lord Buckhurst (here as the earl of Dorset) was said to be of a sweet nature and generous to a fault, scholarly, and valiant, and in all things mannered gently, and he rode a horse better than a gypsy and twice as elegant. He made a fine pair with the king's son, Prince Henry, and they were great friends together. As Lady Anne put it laconically later, he was a 'lover of scholars and soldiers as that, with an excessive bounty towards them or, indeed, any of worth, that he did much diminish his estate'. Lady Anne also pointed out that 'his mother being Lady Margaret Howard, only daughter to Thomas Duke of Norfolk, who was beheaded' (2 June 1572).

Above left: In February 1609, with her match to Lord Buckhurst seemingly settled, Lady Anne danced in *The Masque of Queens*, by Ben Jonson. There were twelve queens; Lady Anne was Berenice of Egypt, whose hair became the constellation *Coma Berenices*. Her costume, pictured, was designed by Inigo Jones.

Above right: Lady Anne here in full court costume as the countess of Dorset.

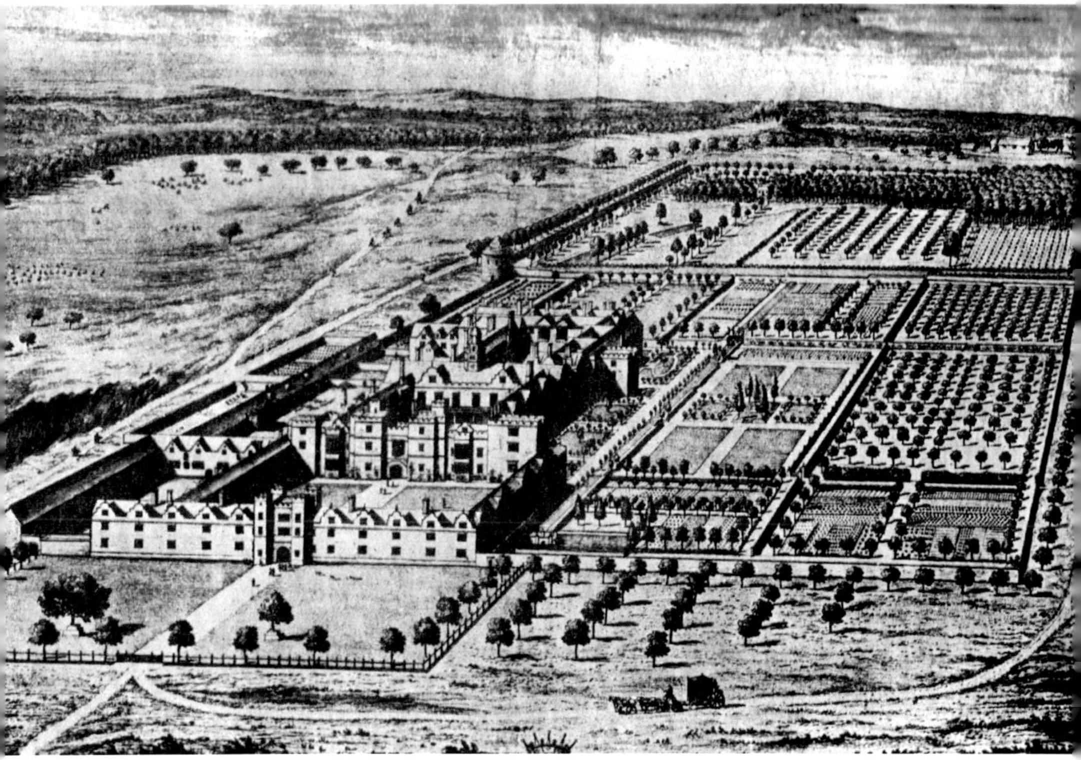

Above: Along with the title of countess, and the husband, came the responsibilities of being mistress of Knole, a vast estate in Kent with a household of over 100. Allegedly there were seven courtyards, one for each day of the week, and fifty-two staircases, for each week of the year, and 365 rooms.

Right: The first child, Lady Margaret, who was to prove such a sterling bearer of children, is here aged four in 1618. She was to become the countess of Thanet.

Above: This portrait of Lady Anne, by William Larkin, was made in 1618 when she was aged twenty-eight and had lost her son, Thomas. Lady Anne gave birth to boys several times but none of them lived; she was pregnant with one of them when this picture was painted.

Opposite below: Lady Anne's first daughter, Margaret, aged fourteen, was introduced to John, Lord Tufton, aged twenty-one, and to say that that their attraction was mutual would be an understatement. The wedding was on 21 April 1629. Their first child was born two years after, by which time the groom was the 2nd earl of Thanet, and Lady Margaret would go on to have eleven more children, only two of whom died young.

Above left: Lady Anne, now with her battle with the king over her inheritance lost and seemingly unable to produce the son and heir so earnestly desired by the earl her husband, was in a depression much of the time.

Above right: Lady Anne's second daughter, Isabella, born 6 October 1622, lived into adulthood and motherhood, marrying a commander in the royalist forces of the Civil War and becoming countess of Northampton.

Contrary to every anticipation, and to the astonishment of the court and all her friends, Lady Anne married Phillip Herbert, earl of Montgomery, and soon to be likewise of Pembroke, in June 1630. He was one of the richest men in the country, so rich in fact that despite every profligate habit, he never exceeded his income.

Above: As we can infer from this painting, the marriage to Pembroke was not a joyous path of roses.

Right: Widowed a second time and her inheritance safely hers at last, Lady Anne decided to make for the north. This picture is much later, when she had established herself as the great lady of Yorkshire and Westmoreland and had achieved most of the works she had set out towards.

Above: During Christmas 1650, Lady Anne purchased a parcel of land below Appleby castle, at the top of Boroughgate, which was to be her hospital of Saint Anne, thirteen alms-houses for widows who were too old or infirm to work, where they would live without rent and be sustained by an allowance. It was against the laws of man, God, and nature not to work if you could, and you had to be very disabled indeed to be judged unfit—unless, of course, you were a member of the aristocracy.

The Appleby alms-houses were finished after five years in the building, and a full set of tenants installed, being 'twelve good women, eleven widows and one injured maid', including one who had a child with her from her marriage to a minister, now deceased.

The rules used to include being in before 9 p.m. when the gates were locked, but that and all the other criteria for tenants have been greatly relaxed although you still have to be over sixty.

Opposite above: Joseph Williamson, later Sir Joseph and a government minister, son of a vicar from Cockermouth, was very anxious to get into parliament. After two failed attempts, he stated his candidacy for one of the two Appleby seats (Appleby was later classed as a 'rotten borough'), with the backing of the prince-bishop of Durham and others. When Lady Anne heard of this, she would not have a stranger in this position and wrote to him to tell him so, saying she had other plans for replacing her late cousin, John Lowther, with a local friend or possibly one of her grandchildren. Of course, she had no direct power to do so, but the few voters of Appleby would surely go with her recommendation. The letter shown is to Sir George Fletcher, High Sheriff of Cumberland, saying the same thing. Thomas Tufton, fourth son of Lady Anne's daughter, Margaret, was duly elected.

Opposite below: Brough castle was put up in the eleventh century on the site of a Roman fort, there to protect the route from York to Carlisle. It was destroyed by the Scots, rebuilt, taken into the Clifford estate, destroyed by an accidental fire one Christmas, rebuilt by Lady Anne, and, like Pendragon, was judged surplus to requirements by the succeeding Tuftons who stripped out anything valuable and left it to ruin.

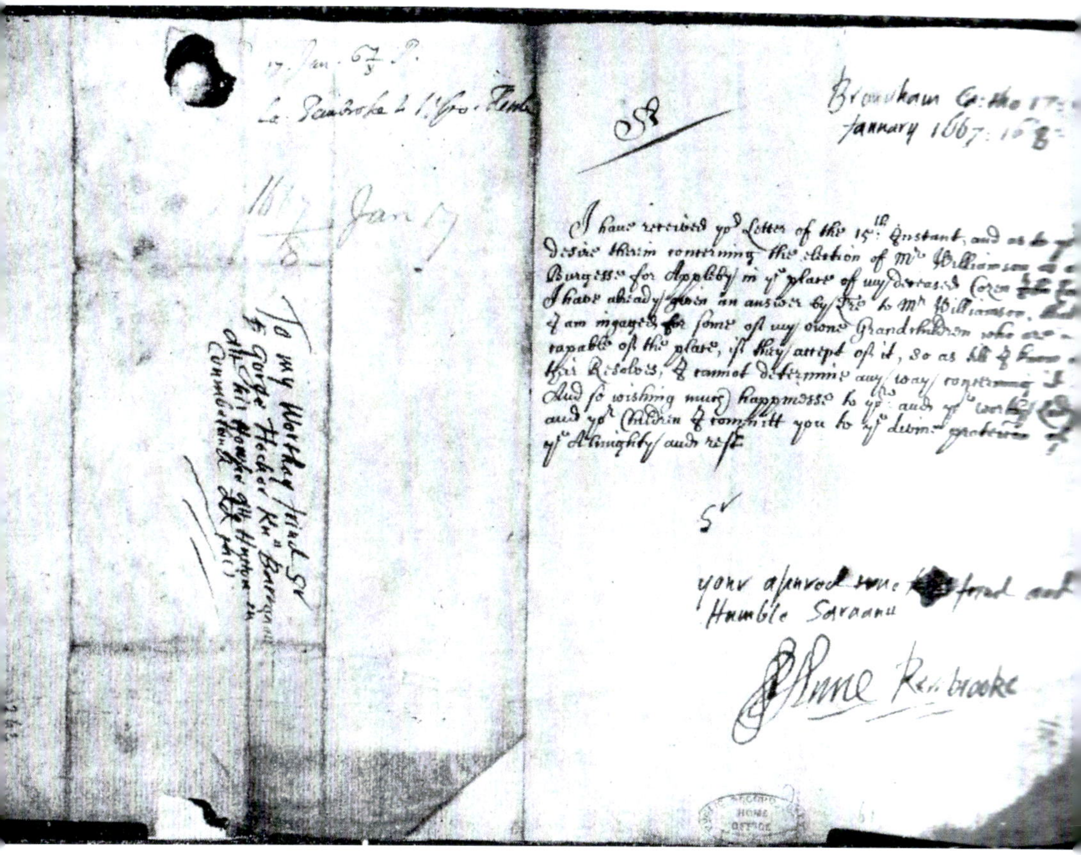

17 Jan. 67/8

Co. Pembroke to Sr Geo. Flet[illegible]

1667/8 Jan 17

To my Worthy friend Sr George Fletcher Knt Baronett att his House att Hutton in Cumberland

Brougham Castle the 17th January 1667:168

Sr

I have received yor Letter of the 15th Instant, and as to yor desire therein concerning the election of Mr Williamson as a Burgesse for Appleby in ye place of my deceased Cozen [illegible] I have already given an answer by [illegible] to Mr Williamson, [illegible] I am engaged for some of my owne Grandchildren who are capable of the place, if they accept of it, so as till I know their Resolves, I cannot determine any way concerning [illegible] And so wishing much happinesse to you and yor worthy [illegible] and yor Children I commit you to ye divine protection of ye Almighty and rest

Sr

your assured [illegible] friend and Humble Servant

Anne Pembrooke

Skipton castle, birthplace of Lady Anne, remains in good shape after many trials, including siege in the Civil War.

Appleby castle, with Skipton the visible legacy of Lady Anne, has changed hands many times and is now privately owned.

A day that would stay in the memory of all of Lady Anne's party was 1 March 1616. She was sure no person had ever attempted to cross those moors by coach before and could not imagine what Dorset had been thinking of when he decided on this route. Perhaps he thought that these mountains were like the Downs of Sussex. It was a most perilous path with no villages on the way, much less towns and inns or houses. Not even a shepherd's hut did they see, and there was scarcely any evidence to say there had ever been a horse or man passing by.

Some miles out of Penistone, they came to the high moors and their horses laboured so that Lady Anne and her women got down from the coach and walked where they could, or rode behind one of the men. Lady Anne rode behind Rivers, but when they came to a precipitous incline, she preferred her own feet, which was as well she did. The men took the horses from the coach and hauled it down the hills with their own hands, while Rivers rode ahead to find out if there was any improvement in the path. Some time passed and they saw Rivers no more, but they heard him later and discovered him standing by a beck with his horse lame, in a steep cut that he could not get out of. The rest of the men made much of this and asked him how he got there, and they were all making jest at his expense for he had been riding across the bridge when he and the horse fell over into the beck.

Should they pull him out, would he turn the trick again for they were sorry to miss it, or should they pull him beyond the bridge so that he would not have to cross it again, he being so unfriendly with bridges. All was resolved and the horse was not much hurt, and they were merry for a while but it became dark and the way was no way at all. Torches were lit, and they thought that perhaps they should leave the coach again and rather ride, but the men promised to find them through and so they did, reaching the inn at Manchester at 10 p.m.

The weather became their enemy in the morning, with rain and mist upon them so that they could see no better than in the dark, and the road north of Manchester was bad. Unlike the day before, they were not compelled to go on for there were towns and villages on the route; they stopped at Chorley, Rivers inquired about lodgings, and could find nothing but a poor ale house. They were in necessity with the weather closed in upon them, and the next day was Sunday. Lady Anne and her women were installed there.

Psalms XXIII: The Lord is my shepherd; I shall not want. He maketh me to lie down in green pastures; he leadeth me beside the still waters.

Lady Anne's rule was always to rest on the Lord's Day, but they could not bear another night at that alehouse in Chorley. Inns varied much in what they provided and their charges did not always bear a strong relation to their provision, but in the case of the Chorley alehouse, all was in perfect harmony. The lodgings were the cheapest in England, and the worst, and this was in times when it was quite usual to have one bed for all, which was so infested with fleas that they were better to sleep in chairs and on the floor. The chamber pots might not have been cleaned since the last persons were there. There could be no food but stale and mouldy bread and hard cheese, although in an alehouse at least the wife could show them the plenty of barrels of ale she had, so they could drink pots of that in defence of their sanity, beyond care if the pots had been washed in recent times or ever.

They were up very early and did not wish to breakfast there so went to the stables and backrooms of the alehouse to rouse the men to get them all to Preston in time for evening church. The roads they found in Lancashire were poor and the inns were still a matter of luck. The one in Preston cannot have been too bad as it deserved no comment either way in the diary, but the one in Lancaster was in the same 'poor' category as Chorley.

They reached Kendal the next night, 5 March, in her own county of Westmoreland, and went out of that inn on the morning and up and across the mountain pass of Shap Fell, and so down through Lowther and to Brougham, where they were greeted with much joy by the dowager countess. It had been nine years since Lady Anne was here, and near two years since mother and daughter were together, which was when the child was born.

Lady Margaret had had word from Lord William Howard and others about the date set for their agreement to the composition, and she agreed there and then with her daughter on their policy, which was absolute rejection of the composition and the ruling of the Court of Common Pleas, with no further discourse required, and spent the day in talk of the child Margaret and the news of the estates hereabouts from the steward Master Clapham.

Some days passed in the wink of an eye, and they heard from Lord William Howard at Naworth, which is hard by the Roman Wall, that his family were now at that castle, which was a good time to see them. His sons and daughters, their wives and husbands and children, were gathered in an army, and Lady Anne would go, stay at Naworth two nights, and then go into Carlisle on her way back to Brougham.

Naworth was the home of the Dacres from the time of Edward III. Lord William Dacre was Lady Anne's great grandfather, whose second son, Leonard, led a rebellion against Queen Elizabeth in 1569, partly through loyalty to Mary Queen of Scots and partly because he felt he had been cheated of his inheritance. The rebellion was acted upon from castles at Naworth and Greystoke, and many came to his flag because of his name, Dacre, which was ever a great name in those Marches, but they were not sufficient to win the cause. There was a battle by the River Gelt, in which the hardened and disciplined soldiers of the Berwick garrison slew many of Leonard's fierce but unfledged Borderers, and he fled to Scotland and thence to the Low Countries where he died a poor man.

The tale has more excitements yet. The reason for Leonard's disinheritance was that, on the death of the then Lord Dacre, in 1560, the duke of Norfolk married the widowed Lady Dacre, and married his own three sons to her three daughters. She had yet a son of her own, but he fell from a vaulting horse that then fell upon him, and he died, leaving all the Dacre lands in the hands of his grace of Norfolk and his newlywed Howard sons, being 70,000 acres of Cumberland, 20,000 of Northumberland, and 30,000 of Yorkshire. Lady Dacre died but a year from her second wedding, and the widower duke was soon entangled in a plot to marry Queen Mary of Scots, the result being his head parted from his body and Queen Elizabeth in a fury seizing all those lands. The said duke of Norfolk thus died in the same way as his father before him and his aunts Boleyn and Catherine before that, which seemed to be one of the ambitions of the Howards.

Of the sons who married the Dacre daughters, one was the said cousin Lord William Howard. After the duke was executed, William had to raise £10,000 to ransom back his lands, which he did by 1602, whereupon he set about restoring peace and good law to the western Marches, which meant defeating and subduing the Reivers.

His success in this was well noted and still is, and many a piratical Armstrong and many a thieving Graham ended on Lord Howard's hanging trees. This form of *Pax Romana* was one side of his nature. The other was scholarly and historical.

After two days with Lord Howard and his many family, during which the business was not spoken of, Lady Anne rode in a coach to Carlisle, there to see the castle. In it she saw the chamber where one of those three Dacre sisters was born, Lady Anne, the one who married Phillip Howard, earl of Arundel, who was a gentleman like to make a fellowship with

Dorset, being directed only to those sports and games which empty purses the fastest. Even so, when his wife converted to a Catholic, Phillip followed and spent thirteen years in the Tower for his faith, where he died.

More days flew by and the hour approached, when they should return their answer. On the 20th, Lord William Howard came to Brougham, in company, and asked that they should deliver up their answer to him, how they received the award of the four great judges. They replied that they should not stand by it whatsoever, that it was not the law speaking but the overweening voice of cowardly men.

At this, Lord Howard was in a passion and a frenzy, for he saw that they had never had any intention of agreeing. He laid about him in language that he might have used in soldiering but which was not of that sort much used in ladies' chambers but rather in the taverns of Carlisle.

So much for Lady Anne's good cousin the Lord Howard, whom Lady Margaret had always mistrusted. He, like all the men in this case, offered much bluster and storm but no solid reasoning nor solving. There was a proverb for such men: there is great cry and little wool, as the Devil said when he sheared the hogs.

On the 22nd, mother and daughter took a coach and went to Whin Fell, which was then kept as a park and still is. They rode everywhere about and through the woods, which were coming into new green for the spring, and were much contented by it.

The ladies had defied the men all, and with good heart, but now their enemies attacked with poisoned weapons. On 1 April, messengers arrived from Dorset to say that he would have staff and horses withdrawn from his wife, leaving her bereft, and her coach was sold to Lord William Howard.

> Psalms CXXI: I will lift up mine eyes unto the hills, from whence cometh my help. My help cometh from the Lord, which made heaven and earth.

The dowager countess gave her daughter's folks a sermon and a call to arms, but they had to follow their lord's orders, and so they went off with a letter from Lady Anne protesting that it was without her consent or desire, that she wished to go with them to London, that she was prevented from doing so by her lord's instructions, and the gentlemen there put their hands to this letter in witness. By doing this, she hoped in some small way to forestall any charges of desertion on her part, for the world would see what it wanted to see, or what it was told it saw. Lady Anne's people returning to town without her could easily be misunderstood, and the gossip could have whistled around that she sent them away, not that they were taken.

This had been Dorset's reaction to the news of their disavowal of the judgement. Lady Anne would not give up her ancient lands for money for her husband to scatter about, and she was condemned for it. Her husband cast her off though he loved her and she him, such was the power of the way things were. They said God ordered it so. Lady Anne said men ordered it so.

One of the messengers was another Howard, Lord Charles, brother to the countess of Somerset, and he related the tale of his sister that she had been taken by water to the Tower on 24 March. She was to be tried for the murder of Sir Thomas Overbury. All the Howards and, for that matter, all the Sackvilles who were close cousins and the like were spattered with the same mud. If her head was to be cut off or her neck stretched by a rope, each family would likely wish to stay away from the centre of the stage for a time.

Other news from London concerned Sir Walter Ralegh, who had been released on the 19th. It was a strange business, for he had promised in return for his freedom to find a gold mine among the Spanish conquests in America, on a mighty river called the Orinoco. The king had made a promise, too, to the Spanish ambassador that should Sir Walter plunder by force of arms against the Spanish, he would pay the penalty, which was death. Possibly Sir Walter would find a way around this dilemma. Perhaps his honeyed words would bewitch the Spaniards into giving him their gold mine at the asking.

Lady Anne's folks, without a coach, set off by the old road for Brough and Stane Moor, expecting to reach Bowes by nightfall, and while they did so, Lady Anne had a change of mind. Cast aside by Dorset and left in Westmoreland would surely signify defeat *in absentia*. Cast aside but being a visible presence in London would mean defying her husband but setting new conundrums for him and her enemies. She sent word after the men, bidding them stay for her, and the message came back from Master Hodgson that they would wait a day at Catterick, on the North Road.

Lady Margaret insisted upon seeing her daughter away, and so they took her coach the next day and went in it as far as they could, which was not very far on that road. They there spent much time grieving over their parting and soaked themselves with each other's tears. Both mother and daughter knew that this separation could well be the last. Lady Anne was going to have to cope with she knew not what whims and fancies of her husband's mind, which, after her refusal of his composition, would surely not include another journey northward.

Time pressed and daughter got down from the coach and took to horse and, while mother was carried back to her lonely fastness, rode on in her weeping with two of Lady Margaret's men, one in front and one behind, and in this way had a fair progress, dinner at an inn at Barnard Castle, and reached Catterick before dark. The horse was a borrowed one, belonging to Lord Howard, and so had to return with those men.

Lady Anne set off for London the next day riding behind Master Hodgson. For sure she had obeyed her husband in sending her folks away, but not in staying at Brougham, she being certain that could not be right and that it was instructed in heat. Had she stayed there, it would have been the end for them, she a lady banished and he a man deserted and a man with a cousin in the Tower for murder. She might have been happy at one minute that he should be pleased with her to have so slid around his peremptory commands, and fallen into hell the next when she thought he might hate her for it.

On 10 April and the ninth of her ride behind Master Hodgson, excepting where she walked, they left the inn at Ware, which is at the sign of the Saracen's Head and has there the Great Bed for twelve people. Lady Anne lay alone in one much smaller. In the afternoon, they were at Tottenham and Lady Anne was much pleased to see Dorset's coach there and to get in it. Peter Baskett, who was the earl's gentleman of horse, was civil to her and showing all manners but was not so warm as she had been used to, and so they went to Little Dorset House. Next they were for Knole and the earl. If Baskett was anything to go by, she must expect a January welcome.

Her dear child, the little Lady Margaret Sackville, met her at the gate in tow of the Widow Benn and Nurse Carpenter, and they were merry and gay for a short while, then went to the drawing chamber to await her lord's pleasure. He came to her when an hour or so had passed and was cold and distant. He was not angry that she had disobeyed him in coming, which she could have taken to mean that he regretted his first fiery orders as being overmuch, but he was not ready yet to show his love for her. She thought it best to be quiet and not to raise any matters beyond his health, and her own health and that of her mother. He left her, saying she should sup in her chamber. She was glad of it, for it postponed the explosion there would be when he demanded yet again that she should sign the papers.

Dorset came to her in her chamber and with no ado insisted she sign the papers. She said to him that she could not sign, for the papers were in

Westmoreland, where she had left them in keeping of her dear mother at Brougham. He, we may imagine, did not speak for a moment, as if he had burned himself on a brand or had a horse stand on a slippered foot, and the pain had rendered him incapable of anything but a staring eye and an open mouth.

When he recovered from his shock, with an adamant wife before him, he could have made his usual list of his wife's defects. She was a trickster, a mountebank, and a dishonest, disloyal shrew. She was an imposter, not a wife. She was a vicious rat in a trap. If she would be a ruler of men, a Cleopatra, she had best find herself an asp. If she would be a Turk, she should wear a turban. She was a mortal sinner for disobeying him and God, she was the serpent in the Garden of Eden, nay, if she had been the original Eve, she would have kept all the forbidden fruit for herself and betrayed her husband, Adam, to the Devil or set the serpent on him.

Lady Anne had known full well what was coming and had prepared herself. It was only words but they gave hurt to her soul, for they seemed to show that Dorset hated her so for this one thing, that it would outweigh the love and tender care he had for her in all other things. She held her peace and protested not at all, when she could have asked him why, if the judges were so agreed, that he needed her hand to their judgement. If the law was clear, there would be no need for her consent, which was to say that it was not clear, and that the judges had given an opinion, not a commandment, and so she might have her own opinion likewise.

The earl, seeing that the covers and curtains on his wife's bed did not set alight with the fire of his wrath and so that his words and ire were wasted, and he left her, vowing to go up to London and never to waste his time on her again.

A week passed with no word from Dorset, when at last Baskett came with a message on the 18th. In sum, the message said that if her lord had asked her to comply once, he had asked her a hundred times, and this was the last of them. Know that he commanded her to write saying that she would fix her name and hand to the award given by England's judges, being prevented only *pro tempore* by the absence of the papers in Westmoreland and her word being taken instead. He would instruct her no more on this matter. He expected her affirmed response without delay, having no wish to send her from him, which he should have to do if she continued in her obstinacy.

If only Dorset had been a more sober and prudent man. If only he had not been so insistent a courtier and a pleasure seeker, he would have fronted Cumberland and his iron son and defeated them. Lady Anne could have given over to her husband all of her estates, Yorkshire and Westmoreland together, had he been the man to make them prosper. They should be living happily for part of the year at Skipton, and hunting from their castle at Barden by Appetreewick, and Appleby and Brougham, and their sons and daughters would have had the Clifford and the Sackville lands together for their inheritance.

As it was, on the 19th, Lady Anne 'returned my Lord for an answer that I would not stand to the Award of the Judges what Misery soever it cost me. About this time I used to rise early in the Morning and go to the Standing in the garden, and taking my Prayer Book with me beseech God to be merciful to me in this and to help me as He always hath done.'

> Ephesians III xiv: I bow my knees unto the Father of our Lord Jesus Christ, of whom the whole family in heaven and earth is named, that He would grant you, according to the riches of His glory, to be strengthened with might by His Spirit in the inner man.

It was done, and Baskett rode with it to London. He was near as good a horseman as the earl, and would be up to town as fast as could be. Lady Anne had to await her fate and would make busy with things as she could, with her dear child and her prayers and the good work of the household, and taking charity forth to those in need, and so she would pass the time.

Word came from London that Master Shakespeare had died at his house in Stratford-upon-Avon. He had written no new plays for two or three years and had become the country gentleman, but not for long did he live away from the theatres. There were others still who made plays but none could match William Shakespeare. The gossip was that Ben Jonson had inadvertently helped Shakespeare to his grave by nights of carousing with strong drink, while visiting said playmaker in his seclusion at Stratford.

9

Torture, Death, Tricks, and a Small Victory

Came May and Lady Anne had letters on each of the first three days of the month, all from London and all of the greatest distaste to her. Rivers brought the first letter, which told her that she should remove from Knole and neither live there nor at Bolebroke, the other Sackville house on the Weald. Next came the steward, Master Legge, whose letter told her that her lord would be coming to see her but that it would be the last time he would do so and therefore it would be the last time they should set eyes upon each other. Next, on the 3rd, came Baskett, and his message said that it pleased my lord to take the child up to London and away from its mother.

Lady Anne fell in a faint of sadness at this last and wept bitterly, at first wishing to fight it but realising that this would make matters worse between them and worse for the child likewise. There was nothing she could do but comply, and so she asked Baskett to send Master Legge to her.

Lady Anne was able to give Master Legge his instructions about the child, and what she should have with her, and whom, and the litter to carry her and so on, and it should leave about 10 a.m. The woman and mother, distraught, reached near to the end of her lecture before a great gulp of weeping welled up again from the bottom of her heart, and her life and her soul poured forth from her eyes.

On the Saturday, the child went to London. Three of the women went with her, and Master Legge with a good company of servants, and Lady Anne must have forced a cheery smile and wished the child happiness until she saw her next, which was a day greatly uncertain in her mind.

Lady Anne took to her chamber with, she thought, no tears left to shed. She wrote a letter to her mother describing the latest, but no sooner was that sent than another arrived from the north telling her that her blessed mother was extremely ill and then another saying she was near death. Lady Margaret would not fear her dying, except that she left affairs unresolved, but her daughter feared it for it would leave her entirely alone in the world.

The news in the letter was five days old, and every day was full of expectation of letters from the north and from London, which would tell that a mother had died and a husband had thrown his wife to the wolves. One came from the earl, which said that the child should live at West Horsley Place, kept by Sir Henry Compton, husband to Dorset's sister, Cecily. Living with them were Lord Edward Beauchamp Seymour and his wife, Dorset's other sister, Anne, and thus little Lady Margaret would have both her aunts to care for her. However, the child would come to see her mother no more, and the mother was to be removed from Knole to a jointure of certain small portions of land and a little house in Sussex, which were to be her means of living when Dorset put her from him, which could be expected imminently. Lady Anne could only hope that this so-called jointure would be free of debts and encumbrances.

How was such a thing possible? How could Dorset be so cruel? This was pure spite and vengeance. No judge would have passed such a sentence upon her crimes, but a husband, scorned and denied his gold, could be so pitiless and vindictive.

Matthew Caldicott came to see her, who seemed to be more consulted and favoured than any other of Dorset's men. This Matthew was like the fat which falls from meat before the fire, which runs everywhere when warm and gives goodness and is much used, but when cold is disgusting and cloying. He was ever cold with the countess, seeming to believe that he was the earl's right hand, which held the sword as well as the pen. She saw him more as her lord's familiar, as a toad or a cat might be to a witch, repugnant but to be wary of.

Matthew had with him a token from Dorset, which was a ring, and it was the ring of his grandfather's wedding, which she took to be a sign that peace might yet be found between them. Matthew said that the child would not be going to West Horsley Place as yet, and that the earl would come to Knole to see her next week. All this seemed more pleasant to Lady Anne than anything she had heard for a long time. She could go to her chamber almost merry, having given to Matthew her own wedding ring to take by return, by which she meant to say that she was Dorset's and her fate was in his hand, which was true of almost all of everything, there being only the small matter of the ancient lands to come between them. There was a great deal else besides for which they should be happy together, and she trusted he would see this in the ring she sent.

Next day, in the evening, Master Gravener came to her, who was gentleman usher to the earl, in high good humour and obviously sent to tell good news of Dorset, to the delight of the countess. This news, of such delight, was that he had won £200 at a cocking match, and that Lord Willoughby and the earl of Essex had followed Dorset's advice and also won large sums, which greatly upset the nobles who had lost to the extent that strong words had been exchanged.

Gravener may have expected that when his tale was complete, Lady Anne should congratulate him, the earl, the lords of Essex and Willoughby and all connected therewith, at their brilliant achievements in winning at a cocking and not killing each other at an insult. She may have had thoughts concerning those who would win £200 one day and lose £300 the next, but thanked Master Gravener for his news and asked if he would kindly express her best felicitations to the earl of Dorset.

More news came to her from other sources, which told her Dorset was much abroad in those days, at cocking matches, horse races, bowling alleys, theatre plays, and all such, where he was acclaimed as the *victor ludorum* and commended by all the world. Lady Anne had to stay at home the while, as in a prison, waiting for her jailer to rattle his keys.

> Psalms CII vi: I am become like a pelican in the wilderness: and like an owl that is in the desert. I have watched, and am even as it were a sparrow: that sitteth alone upon the house top.

On the 13th, Lady Margaret's footman, Thomas Petty, came to Knole bringing letters and news from Brougham. Her folks had resigned up their hopes that she could survive. Her pains and sufferings were near as hard to bear for those around her as they were to herself, and all prayed to God that she recover, or that her most grievous state be ended.

Lady Anne feared that her blessed mother must die and said unto God that she should not, if it was His will, or else He should take her to His bosom without further suffering.

Yet another letter came, this one from Matthew Caldicott, in his own hand, signed by him as chief secretary to the earl of Dorset although

Master Edwards held the title of secretary. In the letter, he bid her ladyship bend to her lord's will, and to comply now or, he said, she should be undone for ever. Perhaps this was but another stone cast at his wife by Dorset, where Matthew wrote at his bidding, his lordship being too proud for any more correspondence on the matter. Or, was Matthew cast in a new role, of counsellor to the countess, to privily beg her to conform for her own sake, as a friend might beg in her interests? Master Caldicott may have possessed many fine qualities which suited him to serve the earl, but to play the part of kind counsellor to his mistress was to ask over much of him, and it was ink and paper wasted.

No sooner had Caldicott gone than he was back. Dorset apparently needed to assure himself that all at Knole was well, in view of the potential motive to indolence that may have overtaken the person in whose charge the house was left. While reports were helpful from his servants, nothing could replace the sight of his own eye. To this end, he would be spending a certain time, not specified, at the Sackville family's seat, and anticipated the opportunity of conversation with the lady of the house, should she find herself disposed to make herself available to meet her lawful wedded husband.

The opposing forces surrounded her after supper on the first night of Dorset's visitation. Dorset began again to rehearse his argument, but he did not dismiss Matthew from the room. Rather, he consulted him at every turn, and asked him if this point was a good one or not, and if my lady was mistaken here, and was it not assuredly the case that God, all the prophets, the Old Man of the Hills, and the Seven Wise Men of Greece entirely would agree with my lord and disagree with my lady?
Matthew was all of these authorities combined and King Solomon had learnt all he knew from Matthew Caldicott.

Lady Anne, alas, had no resort to such a pillar of learning to support her contentions, and so must speak only for herself, which is to say no, and no again, and she will not. And so they parted for the night.

Next day, being Saturday the 18th, Dorset came up with a new scheme with which, for a change, Lady Anne could agree. Her dear mother, the Lady Margaret Russell, dowager countess of Cumberland, was to give over the Westmoreland estates to the earl of Dorset, who in return would pay an annual rent equivalent to their worth and income. Lady Anne saw herself now in desperate times. Her mother was surely on her death bed. The proposal was absurd, out of joint with anything known about the lord of Dorset. He had never been interested in Westmoreland, quite the opposite and, while the income would suffice those of modest expenditure, it would mend only the smallest hole in the smallest sail of the good ship Dorset. If the earl had the estates, he would put the income in his purse, shed it forth again, and there would be no rent paid or, more likely, he would take some cash in exchange from Cumberland for a notional sale, and thus would those lands be lost to Lady Anne for ever.

This was Lady Anne's assessment of the case. She had also to take into her consideration the likely actions of Dorset should she offend him by refusing his demand, and as she wished not to affront him further, she agreed to the scheme and agreed to write a letter about it, knowing that her dear mother would not entertain it in any case.

With the letter gone, Dorset could turn his mind to more pressing matters and so ventured forth with the lords of Vaux, Mordaunt, Compton, and more, and a multitude of knights and gentlemen, to Lewes for a great jaunting there with bull baiting, bowling, cards, dice, and all manner of games.

1 Corinthians IX xxiv: Know ye not that they which run in a race run all, but one receiveth the prize?

Came the message Lady Anne had dreaded. Her dear mother had died five days before, in the afternoon of the 24th. In the very chamber where her husband came into the world at Brougham castle, the dowager countess of Cumberland had left it, and her daughter was alone in her misery. Lady Anne wept and wept, for her mother, for herself, for her child, and for Dorset. It seemed there could never be an end to her distress.

Her mother's will, which the messenger brought, stated that she wished to be buried at Alnwick, where her brother, Francis, was. Lady Anne had thought that it should be Appleby or Skipton, and this threw her into a despair for she saw it as a sign that mother and daughter would have to give in to the men at the last. Her cousin, Lady Wotton, said this was not so, but that her mother would not want to lie with Cliffords at Skipton while there was discord in the family, but Lady Anne could not see it. Only the bleak side of things presented itself in every instance.

Arrangements had to be made, and they were for the conveyance of mother's body to Alnwick and for the building of a little chapel there, while the will was sent down to the earl in Lewes. Visitors came to comfort Lady Anne, but she saw no comfort, and as she was sinking further into a black state of confusion and alarm, a messenger brought a codicil to the will, saying that Lady Margaret wished to lie wherever her daughter chose, which gladdened her heart greatly.

Such gladness could only be a tiny patch of blue on a sodden rainy day until, out of that blue, came a message more welcome than the flowers in May. Dorset was coming home tomorrow and he had an idea about securing the inheritances in Westmoreland. These were Lady Anne's disputed inheritances, her late mother's jointure—previously those few acres of waste land and a scattering of broken castles that no person of quality would want. Dorset wanted to despatch men to Westmoreland to prevent the earl of Cumberland and Henry Clifford from occupying.

As ever with Dorset, there was a strong whiff of self interest in this, but Lady Anne cared not. If the earl made no move to hold Westmoreland for her, and so for himself, her uncle, Cumberland, and his aggravating son, Henry, would seize the lands and pay Dorset nothing for it, and there would be no hope of a composition there.

> Psalms CL iii et v: Praise Him with the sound of the trumpet: praise Him with the lute and harp. Praise Him upon the loud cymbals.

On the same day that Lady Margaret died, Lady Somerset stood before her judges and was arraigned. She confessed her sins and pleaded for the king's mercy, and she engendered pity in all who saw her except Sir Edward Coke, who condemned her to death. On the next day, the lord of Somerset was likewise arraigned, proclaimed his innocence loud and long, and was likewise condemned by Sir Edward.

The lady of Somerset would soon be pardoned by the king but would have to remain in the Tower the while. Her husband had no such dispensation at that time but would eventually, and likewise stayed at that same inn. So we had Sir Thomas dead by a long and lingering death of agony, and those common people hanged who saw to it, and those others who engendered it, and paid for it, were to be let go. If you are to be a murderer, it would be as well to be born of a good family.

Somewhere the hunting horns had been blown, for Dorset came hurling in like a furicano at 7 a.m., said three loving words to Lady Anne and called some more, about taking time by the forelock, as he made haste to his own chamber where he rested until noon. Over their dinner, which they took apart from the rest, he talked without pause of how they must act now and act right to prevent Cumberland from taking what was not his to take. Why, surely this uncle was even then gathering armies to march north and occupy their lands. Letters had to be sent, clarions had to be sounded, and their people had to be made sure that, after being

Lady Margaret Clifford's people, they were now the people of the earl and countess of Dorset and must defend their places as such.

It was both pleasing and an amusement to Lady Anne to hear her estates thus described as theirs. Erstwhile they were barren moors populated by barbarians, but only good could come of this new energy the earl was showing, and there was barely time after dinner for him to approve the texts of various letters which were being written at speed by secretary Edwards, for Lady Anne to sign and seal.

By 4 p.m., Dorset was for London, and she and Edwards were left bobbing and buffeted in his wake, holding on to their letters and papers lest they were thrown in the air or sucked through the door by the wind of his departure.

With a little calm and peace, the two of them were able to tell off the tasks that were to be done, chief among them being letters to her old friend Sir Christopher Pickering of Ormside, high sheriff of Westmoreland, who was acting on behalf of her blessed mother and looking to the estates as needs presented. By Lady Anne's rights according to common law and all precedents, the earl of Dorset should take possession of her mother's jointure, being all the Westmoreland estates and castles. Mother's body was to be wrapped in lead; it was not decided where she was to be buried but in favour was the church of St Lawrence at Appleby.

For three days, Lady Anne and Edwards did nothing more except talk and speculate upon what actions her uncle, Cumberland, might take, then word came from London with her man Rivers that Dorset had sent men north and consulted with lawyers and, upon their advice, had written to Sir Christopher and others, making confirmation of letters previous and asking that all the tenants, officers, and servants of the late dowager countess hold to their posts and possessions and keep all in order in the name of the earl and countess of Dorset.

Lady Anne was delighted at this news. She had been fearful that Cumberland would quietly establish his own people and, in possession, have the advantage if not the law, but she hardly had time to listen to Rivers before her attendant Marsh came in with quite different news.

Her cousin, Henry, had gone with a force of men to Appleby castle and evicted, by his own authority, those men of the earl's who had arrived not hours before. In doing this, he had shivered locks, shattered windows, thrown down doors, and made entry as if he were not Henry Clifford scattering a few servants but King Henry V defeating the French at Agincourt. Marsh said that Lady Anne's husband had heard of all this first and was quite ready to do to the Cliffords what John Clifford the Butcher said he would do to the Yorkists.

Before galloping forth to slay the mighty Cliffords on the field, he took the precaution of consulting the king and the Privy Council, and they were of the opinion that Dorset had the right and Cumberland was in the wrong. It was a strange thing and a puzzle that, nothing more than a few days before, these same worthy gentlemen had been saying Lady Anne had no rights in Westmoreland. Now they said her husband had every right, through her right. Even so, whatever man should give her a horse for nothing, Lady Anne should not be so discourteous as to inspect its teeth.

And so Dorset was triumphant, for proclamations had gone forth from the Privy Council into every corner of Westmoreland that the dowager countess of Cumberland's estates were to be left as they were in her days, until such time as their proper ownership and stewardship were matters resolved in law. The Dorsets waited at Great Dorset House for news of the force of the law and they had not long to wait. Cumberland came to court and prostrated himself before his peers and Lady Anne. Why, nobody had been at Appleby castle for two years. Why, he had believed the earl of Dorset to be nothing persuaded of any virtues in Westmoreland. Why, he had only sent his son, Henry, to secure the castle against malefactors, it being empty, and to guard any possessions there might be belonging to the late dowager and the countess of Dorset.

In which case, they wondered, why was it necessary to eject Dorset's men who were doing precisely that? Why was it necessary to break doors and heads?

Whatever faults Cumberland may have had, taking a whip to a dead horse was not one of them. He capitulated, made his apologies, and escaped without laying blame on his son, which surely was where it lay. Young Henry had no truck with caution and such curbing influences. He would have seen a chance to seize the castle for his father and himself and, without further thought, did so, with orders from father or not. In any case, they should soon be out of it and the Dorsets should be in, but no sooner did Lady Anne's spirits fly high than they were brought low again. The earl, after championing her rights of inheritance and girding himself to slay dragons, offered her another proposal and another lawyer's paper.

It was the same thing dressed another way. She should give over her rights in all her estates to her child, little Lady Margaret. This meant only that she should give them to Dorset, since the child had no rights of her own but all was invested in her father. If Lady Anne were to do this, he could turn Westmoreland into ready money and nothing could stop him.

She said she would not. Lord William Howard was brought in to beat her about the ears with his strong words, but Lady Anne would not budge, and so the earl sent her from him, at 8 p.m., and she had no companion in the coach but Kath Buxton as her other ladies were kept from her, and only the coachman and one footman outside.

In his heat, Dorset thought to make emphasis on his point that Lady Anne would suffer for her disobedience, but he had not thought of the dangers he thus put his wife in. It may have been good daylight when they left but it was dark before they were halfway to Knole and in the deep country. Every shake of a tree and every hoot of an owl brought horrid imaginings, but the footpads and mounted robbers of Kent were abed that night for Lady Anne and her few came home at midnight, fearful, miserable, and whole.

Two days went by and a party of worthies came down from London with the paper again, saying Lady Anne was to sign it, but she sent them away with fleas in their ears, saying she had not yet recovered from her midnight journey forced upon her so suddenly by an ill-tempered husband, and she had no intention of recovering for some while yet. Meanwhile, she would continue to work on her cushion of Irish stitch.

After another two days, the earl himself arrived, with a smile on his face and a more loving tone in his voice, assuring Lady Anne of his best wishes and behaviour at all times henceforth, and how he would be the model of a husband in perfection, the very pattern and paradigm for every husband that ever was and would be. In which case, would she kindly sign the paper? Lady Anne said she would sign a paper, but not that one, but was in general agreement with the proposal.

The earl's objective was to find money or better credit. Money from selling the Westmoreland estates was unthinkable to Lady Anne, but she could go some way to gild the edges of his standing as a debtor. She suggested willing the estates to him, which would help him borrow more, but only so she had no children living, which probably ensured that he would never get the estates. This was indeed a composition, and a happy one for it satisfied all parties without giving anything away. Next morning, they were for London and before the learned justices, and it was decided that Lady Anne had better journey north as soon as may be, to secure her own and to be seen to do so, and to be a surety to her people there that they were secured also.

They went up to court and had kind words with the king and queen and, on the morning of 30 June, Lady Anne took leave of the queen and all her friends in London. Dorset and she were never greater friends than at this time, and he promised to arrange a jointure for her that would allow her to live in good comfort should he precede her to the next world.

10

A Northern Interlude

Lady Anne's mother's death had seemed to be the worst blow that could fall, but it had brought husband and wife together in a way that surely nobody could have foreseen, and they had a loving parting.

After an uneventful journey, ten days later, Lady Anne was in Brougham castle, arranging her dear mother's funeral. Word was brought that the burghers of Appleby town and their mayor had refused permission for the funeral and the burial to be at St Lawrence's, which is the main Appleby church at the foot of the main street. Previously, Clifford women had been laid to rest over the river, in the church of St Michael in the separate parish of Bongate, though the church was in a ruinous state. Lady Anne guessed the seat of this trouble and sent her man Rivers to see the mayor, with an earnest request in the most scholarly and respectful words, begging his permission, and when Rivers came thundering back with a yea, not a nay, Lady Anne's guess was proved. They had only wanted to be asked in proper fashion, as was their invested right, being not a part of the Clifford estate, though the castle was at the end of the street. Theirs was a royal borough of one the size of a village, never recovered from the Black Death and the more ravaging death by the Scots raiders that had reduced the town so.

At about 5 p.m. on 11 July 1616, Lady Anne's cousin, Lord William Howard, and half a dozen of his people arrived from Naworth, and they supped with the household before the funeral procession was put together, with the body in Lady Margaret's coach and four horses, Lady Anne in her own with two, and the rest of the company, being forty or so persons, on horseback. They set forth at 8 p.m. on a fine summer's evening and, at slow pace, made the journey of 10 miles well before midnight. Not one of that family of gentlefolk and servants could avoid a tear, and some were deeply distraught as Margaret, dowager countess of Cumberland, was put in the ground, and all were quiet as they turned for home, which was reached at about 3 a.m.

Quietness was the theme of the next few days, as Lady Anne contemplated her losses and her gains, though all those in the fields were busy enough with working at the hay. Their busy hours in the sun and Lady Anne's quietude in her chamber and gardens were of a sudden equally interrupted by a gang of rough varlets belonging to Cumberland, who galloped into the meadows, ran their horses over the haycocks, charged about the place like boars in the chase, and made noise enough to wake the dead, and more than enough to frighten the women there into hiding beneath the wagon. Two of these brutes attacked a man who had come over from Lady Anne's Appleby farmstead at Nether Hoff to help with the hay. He was a man of stout heart, who had loved Lady Margaret and served her well, and would have defended Lady Anne to the death.

Such sacrifice did not prove necessary, for as the two charged him, he swung his pitchfork this way and that, and put it through the leg of one and the foot of the other. How they cried out and wailed, and called for their fellows to do what they could not, but instead the whole lot of them rode away. The next Lady Anne heard, a complaint had been lodged with the justices at Carlisle and a warrant issued for the arrest of those of her men concerned with the wounding.

Two judges called at Brougham on their way to the Assize, Sir Edward Bromley, baron of the court of Exchequer, and Judge Nichols, revered in near disbelief as the only such who refused to pay King James for his place on the bench. After listening to Lady Anne, they dismissed the case.

Judge Bromley was greatly famed in the region as he who had passed sentence on the ten witches of Pendle, who were hanged in August 1612 at Lancaster. It was said that the evidence was insufficient and that the whole business was something mocking of justice and set up opportunely to please the king, who was a fierce condemner of witchcraft. The modern view of course is that witchcraft is an imagination; in Lady Anne's young day, denial of it was no different to denying the existence of God or the proper divinity of the Protestant church.

Judge Bromley's standpoint was that the jury found them guilty, decisions that were based mainly upon the true and sworn confessions of the accused. Another was acquitted and another was handed a year in the pillory, which was exercise of clemency. Those who were hanged on that day were hanged by an Act of Parliament that stated the sentence. Lady Anne might have wondered what credit there could be in confessions of country women, some as old as eighty and some mere girls, extracted by a torturer paid by results according to a scale of severity, thus a penny for the lash, threepence for the hot iron, and sixpence for cutting a tongue out.

Judge Bromley was also famous for the Salmesbury witches, whom he had tried at the same time but had set free. These five women and two men were accused of turning themselves into black dogs by rubbing themselves with an ointment, which they had made from the flesh of a child. There was no evidence without the accuser's testimony, and by his wit, the good judge had been able to trick the accuser, one Grace Sowerbutts, aged fourteen, into a revelation that she was put up to it by a Catholic priest seeking revenge on an old Catholic family turned Protestant.

With Lady Anne's folk no longer threatened, justice thus was done on all sides and the judges went on their way.

A few days later, a letter arrived by the king's messenger and written in the king's own hand, stating that Lady Anne was not to be molested at Brougham, backing up an earlier letter from the Privy Council to Lord Walden, deputy lieutenant to the Justices of the Peace in Westmoreland, anticipating trouble following the death of the dowager countess and instructing that all matters at Appleby, Brougham, and elsewhere were to remain untouched.

The king's letter also said that things were well at court, and that the earl of Dorset would be arriving in the north very shortly, but did not mention that Dorset had lost 200 20*s* pieces backing his chief footman, Acton Curvett, to beat at running whichever footman or other servant Lord Salisbury, William Cecil, 2nd earl, cared to put forward.

Dorset came north on the 22nd with more horses than had been seen in Appleby in the memory of man, which was where Lady Anne met him and took him back to Brougham in her coach. Appleby must have appeared a very poor place to Dorset, for the county town of Westmoreland. If that was the capital, as it were, of what size and shape would the other towns be? Of more concern to his gaze were the fields. Where were the crops, where were the orchards? There was nothing there but grass. There was indeed a strange, fierce kind of beauty thereabouts, but it was not rich land that a man might make a good living from. His wife's folks must struggle to get the necessities of life, and so to pay their dues.

They came to Brougham in good humour, but Dorset's movables were two days behind and so the house could not be dressed for the new company. They had to take it as they found it, which gave too few beds for too many folk and they had to lie three, four, and five together. When my lord and lady's favoured green velvet bed did arrive on 24 August, it was set up in the chief chamber, the one where her mother had died, the one over the gatehouse, and so man and wife were able to lie together that night in peace and known comfort. The following morning, they were on such good terms that they could discuss Dorset's will, which left almost everything to the little Lady Margaret, saving £3,500 to brother, Sackville, and a provision for paying off debts, which may or may not have been realistic.

The peace was short-lived. Henry Clifford himself came to Appleby on the 26th with a train of folk, not so many as Dorset's but likely to be troublesome. Next day, a Tuesday, there were some ill words exchanged between Matthew Caldicott and some of Clifford's men who set upon him and beat him to the ground. Seeing this, the earl's men, being of the general opinion regarding Master Clifford, allowed the beating to continue for a somewhat lengthier time than was strictly necessary before pushing forward and offering a sound thrashing to any who dared to insult the earl by harming one of his.

At this, two of Clifford's drew their swords, and four of the earl's followed, being Master Edwards the secretary and Master Graverner the gentleman usher and two more, and so more of Clifford's drew, and there was a mighty battle before the church at Appleby. Someone ran for the Moot Hall where he found a ladder and, in the midst of the tumult, put it against the end wall which is topped by a gable in which hangs the bell. He was only a few feet from ringing the general alarm when he fell from his ladder and broke his leg, whereupon some of the womenfolk pulled and dragged him into the Moot Hall and sent for the barber surgeon.

This good man would be busy indeed, for there were three down with sword wounds by the time the leg was broken. That no man was killed was fortunate; that the worst injuries suffered were by Master Caldicott was likewise considered an act of God by those of Dorset's men who later reviewed the high points of the day in this alehouse or that.

2 Samuel XI xv: Set ye Uriah in the forefront of the hottest battle, and retire ye from him, that he may be smitten, and die.

Doubtless wounds were dressed and made much or light of, wagers were paid with honour, tales were told and told again, being longer for each telling, and once more the king's peace settled over Appleby town. Dorset was for Brougham and Lady Anne, where they took a late dinner in their chamber while the earl expounded his theory on Clifford's plan of action. He would want to add Brougham to his possessions, though prevented by letters from the Privy Council and the king. Even so, Dorset believed that such restrictions would only hold so long as Lady Anne was in residence. If she were to be away, Clifford and Cumberland would say that proved she did not care for Westmoreland and they would take possession.

The obvious implication was that Lady Anne would not be permitted to visit London for part of the winter to see her child and all her friends. As for Dorset, he would have to look to Knole, Bolebroke, and the southern portions of the Sackville empire. Lady Anne suspected also that certain courtiers, such as Lady Penistone or another, would be cheering him on the long nights. This Lady Penistone was a noted beauty, wife of Sir Thomas, baronet, one of Dorset's retained thirty gentlemen who, in return for £50 a year (about £10,000 now) and the social cachet of Dorset's favour, would form an entourage whenever required.

Of course, Dorset was itching to be back where he could spend money and live the life an earl should live, as he saw it. Rainy days in Westmoreland spent reading and watching his wife at her embroidery work were not to his taste, and on fine days, the hunting was poor and hard. He would pay a visit to Lord William Howard at Naworth for a few days, then he would set forth from this foreign land and leave it to those who seemingly could exist without courtly pleasures.

Existence for Lady Anne, who would have liked a leavening of such pleasures in the dark days of the year, consisted entirely in reading, being read to, and working at her sewing, after rising early to watch the sunrise as she said her prayers in the Pagan Tower. After some weeks had gone by, she wrote to Dorset asking for his invitation to London, but the reply was a blank no, and so she turned again to her work and her books, a history of the Low Countries, translated from the Dutch, and the essays of Montaigne, translated from the French, both being read to her in English by her gentlemen. Lady Anne was greatly taken also with Plutarch's *Lives*, translated by Sir Thomas North, which was so delved into by Shakespeare for his Roman plays.

11

The Greatest Challenge Yet

Sometimes in the quietest and farthest meadow the sounds of war can be heard, and so it was in Westmoreland in November 1616. While Prince Charles was created prince of Wales at Whitehall, with not so much a pomp as attended his brother, Henry, when he was so created, the most remarkable event at Brougham of this month had been Lady Anne's finishing of a cushion of Irish stitch.

Her husband's brother, Edward, with whom she did not get on, had been made a knight of the bath, and a report from London showed that whenever wealthy young men get together, trouble can ensue:

> On Saturday 9 November the Knights of the Bath were entertained by the Lord Mayor at Drapers Hall with a supper and a play, where some of them were so rude and unruly and caried themselves so insolently divers wayes but specially in putting citizens wives to the squeake, so far forth that one of the sheriffes brake open a doore upon Sir Edward Sackvile, which gave such occasion of scandall, that they went away without the banket though it were redy and prepared for them.

Lady Anne's contemplation of further readings from Montaigne and Plutarch was interrupted by the pleasant task of stringing her mother's pearls and diamonds into a necklace, and a short visit to neighbour Henry Blencowe, when she saw around the house and gardens and heard some music. More dramatic still came overseer Will Punn with letters from London and her lord. It seemed that Dorset had made a challenge to Henry

Clifford, that they would fight, but before they could do so the news reached the king and he summoned them to appear before himself and the Privy Council. The king made the earl and Clifford friends, as far as was possible.

Here the good news stopped, for the king, while dispensing his benefactions upon the two opponents, had further decided to extend his gracious compassion into those affairs between the Dorsets—Lady Anne and the earl—that had proved so troublesome. The king declared that he would make an agreement between them, in royal belief that his wisdom could transcend all quarrels and resolve all matters, and so commanded Dorset to send for his wife. Lady Anne was in delight at the thought of seeing her child again, and her husband, and of passing Christmas at court, but she was in dread of the king's judgement, for surely it would be the judgement of men as all previous judgements had been. The king would wish to be warmed by the flattering thanks of Dorset and Clifford for an accommodation agreeable to them, and would not care a farthing for her opinion or her rights.

> Psalms LVII i: Be merciful unto me, O God, be merciful unto me: for my soul trusteth in thee; yea, in the shadow of thy wings will I make my refuge, until these calamities be overpast.

While Lady Anne prepared herself for her journey and her stay in southern comforts, the earl's man Peter Baskett travelled north with coach and horses. Luckily, he chose to come on the north road, for had he picked a more westerly way he would surely have been prevented at Shap where the pass was blocked with snow. As it was, Baskett could not come through winter's makings at Stane Moor, news of which reached him at Barnard Castle, and so he had no choice but to ride on to Newcastle and take the lowland route that follows the south Tyne and beyond to Carlisle.

Even there, he found himself waylaid by weather. He had to leave the carriage at Rose Castle and thus arrived at Brougham on 4 December 1616, with riding horses only. They set forth on the 9th, making the 20 miles or so to Roses into almost half as much again as they were forced this way and that by the drifts.

Rose Castle at Dalston had been home to the bishops of Carlisle for centuries, although the city of the see was often beyond church's influence. Carlisle itself was Scottish when the Normans came, then English, then Scottish, and such a hard place to govern, and out of sight to both Scots and English kings that it became a place of its own, governed by the ungovernable reivers while the bishops did what they could. The peace brought by King James was then secure enough, though strains could still be felt, when Lady Anne went by. The current bishop of Carlisle was Robert Snoden, who had come in this year after Bishop Robinson died of the plague. Robinson was a Carlisle man, but Snoden was from Nottinghamshire and had been chaplain to the king, and he thought his new diocese was poverty-stricken rather than troublesome.

Passage by carriage proved relatively easy and Lady Anne and her party were in York only three days after leaving Brougham. Leaving York on the 13th, they were in Islington by the 18th and were met there by the earl and a great many in attendance, with Lady Anne's friends in their coaches making ten or more to welcome her and escort her into London and Great Dorset House, where mother and daughter were reunited from their cruel separation of almost a year. Lady Anne's joy at this, and at the earl's pleasant manner with her, was somewhat allayed by an undercurrent of well-meant advice.

All the time of her being in London, she was much visited, and much called to visits, and was the talk of the court. That she and Dorset should be on such good terms was news in itself, but the king's interest in their dispute made everyone more eager to hear all, and at first hand. Lady Suffolk, Lady Northampton, Ladies Gray, Compton, Fielding, Arundel *et alia* came to see her and were of a mind that she should listen to the king and make an end to it.

Lady Anne kept her own counsel in these engagements, and so they dined, supped, played cards, and talked of every other thing that could be talked of, yet still they told her that she must hold to the king's judgement, as if they knew what it might be.

Lady Manners came to dress her hair so that she should not look the country woman at the masque and other festivities, and she also was clear about what Lady Anne should do. Lady Manners was the wife of the earl of Rutland and a daughter of the Tufton family, which would become very closely intertwined with Lady Anne in later years. To complete the new lady of fashion, there was a 'black wrought Taffety Gown' made for her by Lady St John's taylor.

Lady Anne at least felt safe from declarations of royal sagacity so long as the fourteen days of Christmas continued, with their courtly merriments and social obligations. Indeed, it is hard to see from her diary how time could have been found for her case to be tried, as it were, and righteous sentence given.

She returned to Knole on 8 January, and that night, Dorset and she had a falling out about the land. Christmas was truly passed and matters thus returned to form. Lady Anne must now look forward to the king's deliberations and so prepare herself as well as she could. She was not for the block as had been her cousin, Lady Jane Grey, but felt something of her trepidations as the greatest powers in the realm gathered around the throne to hand down their verdict. Still, she had had a memorable and pleasant Christmas.

On New Year's Day, Lady Anne had been at Somerset House after dinner with Lady Carey, who had cared for the young Prince Charles through all his early years, where she met Lady Derby, Lady Bedford, Lady Montgomery, and more of the company that came along with the king, the queen, and the prince. As the king passed by, he kissed her, and afterwards, the queen kissed her and spoke to her very kindly.

Lady Arundel had much talk about the business and would persuade Lady Anne to yield to the king in all things. That night, Dorset was at the play at Whitehall, so she spent an hour or two with her dear friend Frances Beauchamp—that was Devereux—whose father, the earl of Essex, had his head cut off soon after Lady Anne was first at court and Frances was two years old. Now she was wed to William Seymour, late of the Tower and a sojourn in France after his misalliance with Lady Arbella Stuart. Perhaps Frances in the future would have more joy (William Seymour became duke of Somerset and a great commander for the king in the Civil War. Duchess Frances bore him seven children).

On the second day of the year, Lady Anne went to the Tower to see the current Lord and Lady Somerset, being the first time she had seen them since the arraignment. Also for the first time she met Lady Lucy Percy, who lodged there with her father, the earl of Northumberland, which was a strange life for a girl of only sixteen.

This was a pure act of charity by Lady Anne. The earl of Somerset, who had been her suitor when he was Robert Kerr, and his wife that he had taken from the earl of Essex, were convicted murderers and reprieved from the penalty while those whom they had paid to kill had had no such clemency. The Somersets had no credit in the world and rather the opposite, which made Lady Anne's gesture all the more generous for she risked being tainted by association.

The young Lady Percy was in the Tower at her father's bidding, who was Henry Percy, 9th earl, who had been there since the gunpowder treason, although it was never proved that he was a conspirator. Lady Percy, a young woman of great beauty and sharp wits, whose mother was a Devereux, ran errands for the earl, conducted business for him and helped him with his experiments in natural philosophy and alchemy, which mysteries earned him his name of the Wizard Earl.

Chiefly, though, Lady Percy was there to be guarded by her father from matches deemed unsuitable. Most unsuitable of all in his view was Sir James Hay, a Scottish gentleman of little means or estate but a spendthrift and favourite of the king's, whose first wife had died. Alas for the wishes of fathers, his would not prevail while those of a daughter, backed by a king, would, and Lady Percy later became Lady Hay and eventually countess of Carlisle.

On the 5th, Lady Anne attended the creation of Master Villiers that was into the earl of Buckingham. Dorset was one of those who brought him to the king in the king's chamber, which required a degree of stagecraft from the earl, whose grandfather wrote plays and poetry. Dorset saw this promotion of Villiers as yet another of the debases of nobility practised by the king to earn money or to advance favourites, rather than to reward good service, and so he had to hide his opinion behind a pleasant face.

After supper with Lady Arundel, Lady Anne saw Master Fletcher's play *The Mad Lover*, which was put on in the great hall with Master Burbage in the company who was often in the plays of Shakespeare. While Fletcher's tale of man driven mad by misplaced love was diverting, all had to greatly regret the passing of the finest begetter of plays whose work seemingly could not now be equalled, much less surpassed although Ben Jonson came near. His Masque of Christmas that the Dorsets saw on Twelfth Night was greatly better received and mirthful than the sad tale of unhappiness the night before. And so she returned to her own unhappiness, which made greatly worse by love.

The next day, the 9th, had the earl, affronted, reading alone in his chamber while his lady, with apprehensions, occupied herself with small matters. So was business the next day continued, Lady Anne not realising until the afternoon that Dorset had ridden off to London without a word. This filled her with dread. Why would he go without relating his intentions and reasons, unless his very reasons were inimical to his wife?

For six days, Lady Anne sat in anxiety, having a new book about the history of the Turks read to her, it being the first such book in the English language. That something was afoot at court she knew, and that whatever scheme it was, it would not be to her benefit. The king had kissed her at Christmas, but how now was he having his judgement shaped?

> Luke XXII iiil: And while he yet spake, behold a multitude, and he that was called Judas, one of the twelve, went before them and drew near unto Jesus to kiss him.

On Thursday 16 January came a summons to London. The earl said the news could not be bettered, for Lady Anne and he were to appear before the king, for matters between them to be resolved. Lady Anne's heart could sink because she knew which way the dice would fall when the king rolled them. He would incline to the earl, if only because they both were men, and to the Cliffords, where there might be a silver penny or two for regal collection. They were to appear before the king on Monday next, the 20th, but Lady Anne was to make her way to Dorset House tomorrow next day. Arriving there, the countess was informed that the king had changed his mind and they were to offer themselves to the royal presence next day, Saturday.

At Whitehall, on the 18th, Lady Anne went with Lady Derby to the queen, who was promising she would do all the good she could for the countess when in came her excellent friend, the earl of Buckingham, who said she was to present herself at once before the king with Dorset. The queen swiftly gave her a warning that she was not to trust her affairs absolutely to the king lest he deceive her.

The earl and countess knelt by the king, who sent all others from the room, and spoke gently, that they should be at peace and give judgement entirely into his hands. Dorset agreed at once, saying that all those fortunate enough to live under the protection of so gracious a king could hardly do otherwise.

This was all very well, but the trap was open, ready, and baited. The question, it seemed, was not about the lands or Cumberland's will, but about the trust that loyal subjects should put in the wisdom of their own Solomon. Lady Anne thrust a stick into the trap and sprung it, by begging pardon of the king, but she would never part with Westmoreland while she lived. The king, seeing his artifice thus exposed, argued and persuaded, threatened and promised, but she was resolved that nothing would move her.

Dismissed, the couple went back to the queen and eventually home to Dorset House, he being much kinder to her than she had expected, very anxious to avoid any public disgrace through the king's treatment of her.

The next day they drew breath, going only to chapel and to dinner, after which the Ladies Derby, Montgomery and Burleigh told Lady Anne that she should refer the business to the king. They all later went to the masque, but the countess did not as she had seen it.

On Monday the 20th, most of the day went by until Lady Anne was summoned to the king at about 8 p.m. She came into the drawing chamber and felt a chill as the door was locked behind her. Besides the king, there were her uncle, Cumberland; cousin, Clifford; the earl of Montgomery that was Sir Philip Herbert; several more of the Privy Council; likewise of lawyers; and Dorset.

The king spoke and asked all if they would submit to his judgement in this case. Dorset, Cumberland, and Clifford said they would, but Lady Anne said she would never agree to losing Westmoreland.

The king flew into a great rage and chaff, and Pembroke spoke much against her, as did Sir Randal Crewe who was the king's solicitor who was supposed to speak on behalf of Dorset and herself. Dorset did his wife a great courtesy. Fearing that the king in his temper would say words about her before this distinguished assembly that could not be retracted, he bade Sir John Digby open the door. Sir John was the ambassador to Spain and sought to marry the Infanta to Prince Charles, and so was trusted with the highest diplomacy where much gold was depending. He let them out, but his silver persuadings beyond the door brought him no reward and word was later sent to Lady Anne that the matter was resolved—that if she would not come to an agreement, there should be an agreement made without her.

Lady Anne could not believe this could be so, but if it were to come, it could never be said that she surrendered to those whose strengths so far exceeded her own. She believed that her husband, eager though he was to reach his composition, would not countenance it without her.

There were also more mundane difficulties to attend to, and on the 22nd, the child took a fit of the ague, which was the sixth time. How helpless mothers were in such matters. The learned doctors delivered wise words on the causes and the course of these shiverings and sweatings, which seemed to last forever. Mother did not know the cause, and neither did the doctors, and for the lack of anything other, she prescribed the medicine, which was betony tea, and followed the advice of her women, which was to put salts in the child's beer.

At home in Knole, Lady Anne sent her husband a letter thanking him for his kind behaviour in London, and telling him of the child's ague, he rode down to see them that afternoon. The earl's better instincts, in removing his wife from the king's wrath, might have put him in a parlous case. Viewed through the eyes of enemies, he could be said to have defied the king, which is to say God's right hand on Earth, or at least to have criticised or obstructed him. Dorset's stratagem in turn was to keep close to the king in the succeeding days and to ensure that, in cocking matches at the Whitehall pit, the king's birds won rather more than they lost against Dorset's.

While all was expense and high life at court, Lady Anne at home had little excitement. Occasional visits from Dorset interrupted the routine of reading, writing letters, walking in the gardens, playing cards with her steward, sewing her cushions in Irish stitch, and the daily care of the child who was much recovered in health by the beginning of March despite several fits. News from London varied; these courtiers were on her side and believed her mistreated, while these other courtiers thought her wilful, obstinate, and worse. Sometimes, Dorset was in a bad mood with his wife; sometimes he was the good husband he had once promised to be. Still there was no pronouncement on her lands, which gave her hope, and there was a kind of peace at Knole, as on a cloudy day, but things were coming to head in London.

On 22 February, Baskett came for some horses as the earl needed them for his ride out with Prince Charles, and while he was there told Lady Anne the latest. The king was going to make a composition to put her from her rights to the land, so she must consider matters speedily or it would be too late, for the king was firmly against her. On the 27th, a letter came from Dorset saying the king had referred his decision to the solicitor general for drafting into legal terms.

More days passed, in bible readings, needlework, caring for the child who now had eighteen teeth, saying prayers, and going to bed early for want of anything else to do, until Baskett came from London, on 15 March, and announced that Dorset and Cumberland were agreed and the writings sealed. This they viewed as a conclusion, cutting her off; Brougham, Appleby, and the rest were to be occupied by Cliffords. There was nothing Lady Anne could do but deny their right, which she would ever do. They were trespassers and would not be forgiven.

The king left for Scotland on this same day, leaving no reason for the earl to stay in London at an empty court, but he did not come home to Knole where, being in general unwell, he might have been better looked after. Instead, he went to Buckhurst, and called for his horses and his hounds but not his wife. When he did come to Knole, he was still afflicted with coughs and malaises, which was no help to his mind when he tried to explain to Lady Anne that she had not been written out of things all together.

Matters were finished, and yet they were not. Dorset in a foul temper told her she had no money left; in a good mood, he would come to her chamber for the night. On 6 April after supper, because he was sullen and not willing to go into the nursery, she had a servant take the child to him. Then he fell ill, and Lady Anne fell ill, and he tried to persuade her to go up to London to sign her name to the composition, so far undefined, and on the morning of 17 April, he told her that he had entirely given up any further attempts to move his wife on the matter. On the 19th, Easter Saturday, he spent all evening rehearsing the same arguments and persuasions, with the usual result—a resolute denial and a great falling out.

The next few days alternated between good relations and bad. The great falling out was on the 20th, Easter Day; on the 22nd, they dined together and played bowls; on the 23rd, they slept apart after another fall out; and on the 24th, they played bowls and he came to lie in her chamber. A few days' hunting followed for Dorset, down in Buckhurst, while Lady Anne proudly put on the child's first grown-up coat, of lace and red baize, over a whalebone bodice.

Dorset was in even more financial difficulty than normal and was selling off pieces of the estate, some to his brother, and in late May came some more unwelcome news. Master Woolrich, steward at Brougham, had come from there being no longer needed by the Cliffords, with some of Lady Margaret's things and a great many books that he and Lady Anne set up together, happily and sadly talking of old times, when a letter arrived from her cousin, Russell. Dorset himself had not written for several weeks, and Lady Anne had responded in like manner, but this letter would need a reply. It said that Dorset had cancelled the jointure settled upon his wife the previous year. The footman, who brought that letter, also told her that the papers of the composition were to be signed and sealed the next week.

Lady Anne wrote to her husband, saying how ill she took it that her jointure should be cancelled but expressing her willingness to bear it as he thought fit, meanwhile thinking that her enemies may have believed they had the upper hand, and her husband may take his revenge upon her, but she should bear all with patience under the eye of God.

> Proverbs XVIII xiv: The spirit of a man will sustain his infirmity; but a wounded spirit who can bear?

Being out of her year's mourning for her mother, during which she wore only black and white, and resolved not to be cast down, Lady Anne had two new gowns made, one of sea-green satin and one of damask embroidered with gold, which had open ruffs after the French fashion. Most of the days of June were spent in quiet pursuits, with two indifferent letters from the earl to add nothing nor take anything away. He was in London for a christening in the Howard family, which would bring him close in to his scheming brother, Edward Sackville, and to Prince Charles. For a reason that Lady Anne could not explain, this filled her with foreboding and, as if fulfilling a prophesy from a witch, a letter on 2 July told her that the earl had willed all his property to the brother, and another on the 9th told her that the king's award was finally sealed. She and little Lady Margaret were lost.

The document of the award was brought to her on 9 July, and she spent the next few days studying it. It began by setting out the circumstances of the various disputes that had been brought forward for the king's princely consideration, and noted that the several parties had agreed to abide by the king's decision, Lady Anne's agreement having been made on her behalf by her husband.

All the lands in Westmoreland and Yorkshire would come to Francis, earl of Cumberland, and after his decease to Henry, Lord Clifford, and his male heirs. In default of such heirs, the estates would come to the earl and countess of Dorset for their lifetimes, and on to Lady Anne's first son, or daughter if there were no son. If there were no daughters, all would return into the Clifford family.

In return, the Cliffords were to pay £20,000 (about £3.5 million today) to the earl of Dorset, in pieces, thus: £5,000 at Michaelmas next; £6,000 on the feast day of the birth of St John the Baptist 1618; £6,000 on the same day in 1619; and the remaining £3,000 on Michaelmas 1619. Further, the Cliffords were absolved of the responsibility of paying the original £15,000 left to his daughter by George Clifford, not a penny of which had she ever seen.

Should Lady Anne survive her husband, she should not bring the matter to law again or she would have to repay the £20,000 and suffer other penalties.

Quite where the Cliffords were to get the £20,000 to pay Dorset was not of course specified, but it would have to have been by raising loans and charges against the estate, which would greatly encumber any subsequent owner with debt. Lady Anne's mother's possessions at Brougham and Appleby had been variously placed in safe keeping and the servants there employed or dismissed.

So, it was all over. The matter had been settled by divine right. Well, at least there would be no more quarrelling, for a day or two at any rate, and Dorset did seem more kindly disposed towards his wife, perhaps out of sympathy, although he did not stay long.

He went away for two months, on a kind of progress through the lands of his influence, hunting, at the races of Lewes, and elsewhere, enjoying a great many gatherings of fine folk, lords, and ladies, while his wife suffered a summer of tedious times and much sadness. One highlight was late in

July when Lady Anne went to church morning and evening to hear Doctor Donne preach (John Donne the poet), who had become rector of Sevenoaks, not having found the position at court he wanted (he became dean of St Paul's in 1621). He came after to dinner in the Great Chamber and amused the company, which was a merry interlude in those wearisome days.

There was a cause for celebration, in that Lady Anne was sure she was with child again. Should she bear Dorset a son, there could be no question of his leaving his estate to his brother, a matter that itself seemed resolved when a rumour swept about that brother, Sackville, had fought with Sir John Wentworth and been slain, but this rumour had no substance.

Lord Keeper of the Privy Seal Sir Francis Bacon, *pro tempore* regent of England and Wales while the king was in Scotland, had been living at Dorset House. When he left his own quarters, the earl would have the place set about and put to his liking again, which was, he said, the concern of his wife. She refused, not being so well disposed yet towards him that she might take on such burdensome work.

The king, on his way back from Scotland, had been hosted most royally at Brougham castle by the Cliffords. A specially composed musical entertainment had nine songs written exclusively for the occasion, with titles such as 'Welcome, welcome, King of guests' and 'Truth sprung from Heaven shall shine', performed by a company of singers brought up from London. The Cliffords wanted to show the king their gratitude for his role in the composition.

On 29 September 1617, the earl of Dorset returned home from his jolly tour. It was Michaelmas day, and according to the composition, he should have had the first £5,000 of the payment. In fact, he had £4,000 to bring with him; perhaps the shortfall was due to necessary disbursements to creditors. In any case, they were merry together, and there would have been a private dinner of goose, and with it Michaelmas pie or dumplings with the last blackberries of the season. The Devil was supposed to have spat on them after that date, the date he fell to earth and landed in a blackberry bush. Lady Anne had also made a great store of jars of quince marmalade, which she used as presents for her visitors.

Dorset, in good humour, would have been solicitous for his wife's health and so of his son and heir, and attentive that nothing should want between now and the birth, which was expected to be well into the next year.

> Isiah VI xiv: Butter and honey shall he eat, that he may know to refuse the evil, and choose the good.

Another challenge was on the horizon, in the shapely form of one Lady Penistone, with whom Dorset was now consorting quite openly, and this scandal made Lady Anne much less willing to go to court although she had to come up to London for Christmas, which came and went with the usual round of feastings at Dorset House, which Lady Anne attended as she could, glad that the most constricting of stays, farthingales, and such like were no longer the fashion, so she could wear her new gowns with more comfort. The earl lost £400 at cards with the king, little Lady Margaret recovered from a smallpox scare, and they all removed to Knole as soon as Twelfth Night was over.

The new child was waited for but did not meet the hour expected. Lady Anne's calculations were out, or the infant was in no hurry to join the world, but on 2 February at last came the boy, hale and bold, and he was christened Thomas after the first of the modern earls of Dorset, he who was a close comforter of Queen Elizabeth and died of a fit at the Privy Council.

There were many difficulties with the boy's nursing and several different women of the village were tried until one could be found whose functions were consistent. This woman, whose child had died within a few days of birth, was glad to give her milk to the little Lord Buckhurst for a wage exceeding that her husband could get as a herdsman.

Lady Anne had fed Lady Margaret herself, as was her preference, but giving the nursing over to another was often done in great families, for the man would want his wife ready for another pregnancy as soon as may be. As with the cows in the field, if they are not milked, their supply dries, and this, in womankind, brings on her monthly cycle the quicker.

Matters did not continue well, however. The boy fell more and more into sickness and the earl seemed to lose interest in his heir, as the physicians plied their trade to no good effect, and it showed more likely that this, at least, was not the future Dorset.

The end came on 27 July 1618, when he cried his last and his pain was relieved. Lady Anne could not know how to pray, nor how to speak with her husband, when one child died while she had another within her, which should be born before the year was out. What could she hope for this time? Was there hope at all, for anything?

> Job XIV i: Man that is born of woman is of few days, and full of trouble. He cometh forth like a flower, and is cut down: he fleeth also as a shadow, and continueth not.

The combined gloom of the child's death and of the king's award did not pass, and Lady Anne could not be cheered with news from London, although interested to learn that there would be no more masques from Ben Jonson for a time, as he had set forth for Scotland, the land of his ancestors, and meant to journey on foot.

Regardless of mood, Lady Anne steadily grew larger, with another child in her belly, while the earl was too occupied to pay much heed. For most of the second half of 1618, she kept to her chamber with the curtain closed against the light, while the earl largely stayed at court. As winter itself drew in, her spirits fell into an even deeper slough, with the earl only occasionally making some attempt to alleviate her sufferings, or at least to bring the latest news.

On 29 October occurred the execution of Sir Walter Ralegh, who had been in the Tower since 1603 at the king's behest, unexecuted despite his trial finding him guilty of treason, which merits the block. The golden city had proved as insubstantial as was his promise not to step on Spanish toes, which the king must have known could not be kept. Sir Walter fell ill on the Spanish Main and sent his men up the river and they, seeking El Dorado, found a fight in which was killed his son, Walter, and a number of Spaniards.

As much as Sir Walter knew his success in finding gold was bound to falter without a miracle, so his return home was bound to end with the axe. The Spanish ambassador, one Gondomar, demanded it and the king gave it, but sought to avoid popular upheavals by having it done privately. Rather than crowds on Tower Hill, there were but a few witnesses, among them Dorset, in the Old Palace Yard at Westminster.

Sir Walter had been eager to have the business concluded, and examined the axe to be sure it was fit for its work. He spoke, saying that this was a sharp medicine but a good, as it cured all diseases and miseries, and bid the axeman strike. There were instructions from Lady Ralegh—that was Bess Throckmorton and lady in waiting to Queen Elizabeth—to embalm the head for her to keep. It is sure that they were a loving couple beyond the usual, enough to spend years together in the Tower and, indeed, to risk the queen's displeasure by marrying without her consent, and to confirm it by having a child so soon after wedlock.

There was a visit to London and to court in November, when the queen sent for Lady Anne to her bedchamber, where the king was also, who was well satisfied with his trial, judgement, and sentence regarding the business, confirmed in finality by Cumberland's first payment. The king therefore could afford to be most gracious, bestowing a kiss upon her and even suggesting that she should go to Gray's Inn to see the king's own attorney, who would be willing to explain the many legal intricacies that perhaps Lady Anne might not yet understand. She thanked the king for his kindness and left unsaid her thoughts. She was defeated, for the moment, and not well, she hoped for the moment, but while she had to admit to the poor health, she would never admit to the defeat.

At court at that time, the earl and the countess could have seen the play of Master Fletcher, done by the King's Men, called *The Loyal Subject*. Audiences wondered how the master of the revels allowed it, as it was surely a reflection of England under King James and not a flattering one. Some of the players were well known, such as Burbage and Condell, but without Shakespeare, they did not have the good silk with which to embroider their art as they used to do.

On 20 December at about 10 a.m., Lady Anne was delivered of a boy child who died soon after. Lady Anne may have expected her husband, whom she loved despite his many faults and who professed love for her, to be with her in such distress but he found Christmas at court too much of an attraction.

Far from inducing a return to her dark moods, this loss and rejection served a good purpose, in that Lady Anne made a fresh resolve to put a brave face on all matters and to keep up her strength and will as the year turned.

She began to have the curtain drawn in her chamber to see the light and little Lady Margaret put on her crimson velvet coat with silver lace, which was the first velvet coat she ever had. Lady Anne sent the queen a new year's gift, being a cushion of cloth of silver embroidered with the king of Denmark's arms, and on 2, 3, 4, and 5 January, many friends came to see her to console for the loss of her child and to tell her the news she had missed during her confinement, the most important being that the queen was grievously ill. The queen had not stirred from Hampton Court all Christmas and had been thought at times certain to die.

Lord William Howard of Naworth had brought a grievance against Henry Clifford and made him appear before the lords of the council. While the grievance itself was not really of interest to Lady Anne, the strife and spleen between the Howards and the Cliffords could only do her cause good, for if they were united in accepting the composition and matters as they then stood, in peace and good will, she should never regain Westmoreland. There was also talk of unrest among the tenants that the Cliffords used them badly and did not keep to the proper tenancy terms.

Otherwise, all the news was of sickness. The queen lay at Hampton Court still, and the earl had to stay in London a week longer than he planned, falling ill after riding there through snow too deep for a carriage. The king suffered an extreme fit of the stone and colic, which the doctors said was caused by the stone leaving that vessel in the body which holds the bile, while such stones were caused by excesses of rich food and wine. The pain in the fit was of the worst, but sometimes might herald a release, and indeed, the king voided a stone in his stools the next day.

By 2 March 1619, Queen Anne, who had been Lady Anne's friend in her trials, was dead. She had been long ill and much destroyed in herself, which was the burden of a woman, even though she was a queen, who bore seven children and dropped more that never came to birth. Margaret died not two years old, Robert but a few months, Mary was two years, and Sophia one day old. Prince Henry died at the age of eighteen, Princess Elizabeth lived on with her husband, and Prince Charles was to be the next king.

> Job I xxi: The Lord gave, and the Lord hath taken away; blessed be the name of the Lord.

The queen's corpse was brought by water from Hampton Court to Denmark House, with many lords and ladies attending in the barge. That was at night, and earlier in the day, the queen's entrails except her heart were buried privately, with few attending, at the abbey of Westminster in the place where the tomb is of Mary Queen of Scots.

Letters from the earl and from Master Smith the physician persuaded Lady Anne not to keep so strictly to her Lenten fast, and not to forswear butter and eggs as she had been doing. Eating no meat, but only herbs, vegetables, and salt fish, had left her very pale, weak, and sickly, and liable to sudden great passions of weeping, and not fit to receive the communion at Easter.

Meanwhile, the earl recovered his health and so could go to Royston to visit the sick king, it having been pointed out that every other great man had done so. He and Lady Anne met in London for a few days of making calls and catching up with friends, some of whom were in the Tower. On 19 April, Lady Anne took her turn to sit by the queen's corpse during the day, and again on the 23rd for the whole night. On Sunday, Lady Anne went to church to hear the sermon, and on Monday, the earl put a dozen cocks into the pit at Whitehall.

Their stay in London was prolonged, in expectation of the queen's funeral, and so they were in town for the execution of Williams the lawyer, who had been condemned for treason and adjudged to be hanged, drawn, and quartered for a certain book he had made and entitled *Balaam's Ass*. Dorset and Clifford saw him carried from Newgate to the Mews at Charing Cross where he met his death bravely, saying *Post tenebras spero lucem* as a Roman Catholic, these words meaning 'after the darkness I hope for the light'.

This Williams, although a barrister of the Middle Temple and a member of parliament, had acted foolishly. He was sent from parliament for being a Roman Catholic, and he was much exercised by his beliefs in the wrong directions that the country was taking. He wrote his poem, *Balaam's Ass*, also called *A Free Discourse touching the Murmurs and Feared Discontents of the Time*, in reference to a small part of a long and complex story in the Book of Numbers, in which an angel makes an ass talk and opens the eyes of the foolish and false prophet Balaam to the truth. It was open to interpretation whether King James was cast as the ass or the prophet, though surely he was not the angel. In the poem, Master Williams stated that the king, according to words in the Book of Daniel, would die in the year 1621.

Somehow this poem, which was never printed and of which there was only one copy, and which was 'directed to his then Majesty King James' although never meant for his eyes, came to the notice of the king and there was only one possibility from thereon.

It seems that Dorset and Henry Clifford were good companions at this time, 'going to Hyde Park and those places' as Lady Anne put it, which did not please her and was only offset by another, more powerful cousin, Lord William Howard, who was ever rumbling about the ruffianly doings of the Cliffords in the North.

On the 13th, Lady Anne was among the mourners at the funeral of the queen, which was a very great affair. She walked hand in hand with Lady Lincoln from Somerset House to the abbey. Dorset walked also, and Henry Clifford carried a banner of arms. They buried the queen not then, but after all had gone except for 180 poor women mourners. The doors were locked, and the dean of Westminster and others performed the interment in the chapel of Henry VII. Lady Anne's mourning attire was 16 yards of broadcloth as set down for her rank.

That night, Dorset gave a great supper for certain of the Frenchmen who were with the ambassador, and a supper for many lords and ladies, with a play between called *The Humorous Lieutenant*, written by Master

Fletcher and performed by the King's Men who had been barred from such while the queen lay dead. They applauded the play but were sorry to miss Master Burbage in it, who had died.

Lady Penistone was there, which was the first time she had been in Lady Anne's house, but they spoke little. Sir Thomas Penistone, one of Dorset's retinue, paid back some of his gratuity of £50 a year as rent for a Dorset property, Lordship House, in Tottenham. Sir Thomas was a lawyer. His father was a wool merchant and his wife was deemed most dainty in her looks, an appraisal with which the earl of Dorset agreed.

All the household went down to Knole on the 17th, delayed by two days for the rain, and that night, the earl came to Lady Anne's chamber. Perhaps Lady Penistone was in his mind.

Two tenants at King's Meaburn in Westmoreland came to London to lose their case against the earl of Cumberland, Lord Chancellor Bacon telling them to rein in their dissent and do as Cumberland bid them. If matters had been right and they had been Lady Anne's tenants, those good men would have had no need of a case. She gave them money but could not give them justice.

Her cousin, Lord William Howard, put a bill into the Star Chamber against Sir William Hatton and others of Clifford's faction, which at least stirred up the dust around the business, while Dorset attended cocking matches with the king but, for a change, won a great deal of money.

On the last day of May, Lady Anne was overcome with melancholy and was very sad. She told her husband that he was good to everybody else and yet unkind to her, at which he said he was to make a jointure to her of £4,000 a year. His calculations included the Westmoreland estates, but he did not say how he would wrest these from Cumberland.

The summer of 1619 was a bleak one for Lady Anne. The highest point was little Lady Margaret's fifth birthday; among the many low points were unpleasant letters and words from the earl, who spent all his time at sports, sometimes in the company of Lady Martha Penistone who took the waters at Tunbridge Wells all that while. As for the business, there were mixed fortunes. The earl had the second-last payment of the composition, being £6,000, which made £17,000 all told, with three remaining due at Michaelmas. This last part, according to the king's decree, he could not have without Lady Anne's agreement to the composition, or an Act of Parliament, and so he never did have it.

Henry Clifford's wife gave birth to a son, who would have been heir to all the estates and the title of earl of Cumberland, but it died in hours.

By the autumn, Lady Anne was ill, melancholy, and with child. She retired to her chamber, where she could have people read to her and visit her. The latest tale running among those who talk of such things was that Dorset had put Lady Penistone from him, visiting her at her mother's lodgings in the Strand for the last time. Such news could not cheer as rather than being a sign of a new resolution and a reformed character, it was bound to mean only that greener grass has been spied over yonder hill. Dorset's new grazing was said to be among beauteous lilies indeed, with a girl of only nineteen years, Venetia Stanley, daughter of Sir Edward Stanley of Shropshire, who was at court with only her maids with her.

One evening in November, after supper, Dorset and Lady Anne had a great falling out over the same subject as ever. She said again that though the matter was closed in his and everybody else's eyes, it is not so closed in hers and she would not agree to his composition while she lived. The earl said that the lands would not come to her while she lived either.

Dorset would spend Christmas in London. Lady Anne would spend it in her chamber at Knole. She had not crossed the threshold since October last and would not cross it for a time yet. Her third son, to be called George for her father, died before he could be christened, and so the earl's brother, Edward, stayed heir to all. She and her husband remained at a strain, though the sun may have shone occasionally and they may have loved one another as they used to do. In a black depression, she could only see the darkest clouds and the foulest winds in her mind, and she would not draw the curtains to look out. News came from London that Martha, Lady Penistone, had died of smallpox and had been buried at Stowe.

A daughter, Isabella, was born on 6 October 1622, but still Lady Anne was lost in her mind as in a dark mist, and only the care of Margaret and the new cares of Isabella kept her from utter despair in the times following—and what times they were.

The earl, although only thirty and some in years, was increasingly sick while refusing to slow the pace of his extravagances. He was the champion squanderer of the age, a reckless prodigal who indulged in all things that money could buy until there was no money he could find, and then carried on regardless.

His debtors became more insistent, and to meet their demands, he leased almost all of the Sackville properties and sold them when the proceeds proved insufficient. Without telling his wife—although she found out—he even tried to sell Knole from under their feet. He had been left a great fortune, yet in only a few years had managed to consume all but a very little, and the very little was less than nothing if matched against the debts.

On 10 July 1623, the earl, in Great Dorset House, being then very sickly, made over to Lady Anne for her jointure certain lands in Sussex, part of which she would make over to her two daughters, subject to the researches of lawyers to assure her that there were no debts or encumbrances hidden away. If so, it would be her own business to see that none such became attached by a side road.

Came Christmas at Knole in 1623 and the earl was too ill for court, and so he had to spend all the days of Christmas at home. The obligations of the greatest nobleman in the county, and one of the greatest in the country, were such that expenditure could scarcely be believed. The earl, conscious of matters *in statu quo ante* and of popular expectations, made sure of a lavish reception to all in an open house, from Christmas Eve to Epiphany, with the house dressed in holly, ivy and mistletoe. Although he was not in health enough for revels, he put on a brave show and met as many of the local nobles, gentry, clergy, and tradesmen as he could, who came in their hundreds whether needy or not, and where he could not meet, Lady Anne filled his place. Those classes of folks below, even including beggars, were also attended to. Mummers and wassailers came and went, and all those sorts of person in festive garb, and they saw those pleasant practices that the Puritans were wont to crush but which they could never do in the far country, although they had partial success where the law could easily reach.

As always, gifts were exchanged on New Year's Day, between countess and earl, and from master and mistress to those more important members of the household, and from mother and father to daughters, although Isabella was too young to understand.

There were brief times when the earl recovered and was himself again, but this would prove to be their last Christmas together. Lady Anne fell ill too, and little Lady Margaret; they were at Knole while the earl had gone to Great Dorset House and could move no further for his fits of vomiting and fever, so they were apart when the moment came. Lady Anne kept the last letter Dorset sent to her, which he wrote on his last morning on this earth, being Easter Sunday 1624. By the time she received it, her husband was dead.

26th March 1624
Sweet Heart,
I thank you for your letter. I had resolved to come down to Knole, and to have received the Blessed Sacrement, but God hath prevented it with

> sickness, for on Wednesday night I fell into a fit of casting, which held me long, then last night I had a fit of fever. I have for my physician Dr Baskerville and Dr Fox. I thank God I am now at good ease, having rested well this morning. I would not have you trouble yourself till I have occasion to send for you. You shall in the meantime hear daily from me. So, with my love to you, and God's blessing and mine to both my children, I commend you to God's protection.
> Your assured loving husband, Richard Dorset.

Dorset died owing £60,000. In his will, he left 'to his dearly beloved wife all her wearing apparel and such rings and jewels as were hers on her marriage, and the rock ruby ring which I have given her. Also my carriage made by Mefflyn, lined with green cloth and laced with green and black silk lace, and my six bay coach geldings.'

These and other goods were in addition to her jointure and the £4,000 a year, although where that was to come from was not indicated. Not mentioned in the will, but of immediate concern nevertheless, was the fate of two of Dorset's children that were not born to his wife. These were girls, aged nine and seven, of high birth but unacknowledged, who needed a home and a family more than anything in the world. We cannot know quite what would have become of them had Lady Anne not taken them under her wing. She would never say who the mother or mothers were, but we must know that it was not Venetia Stanley, who had £500 a year from the earl and who married Sir Kenelm Digby, and took with her own acknowledged children and her annuity. The new earl, Edward Sackville, later tried to stop payment but Sir Kenelm took him to the courts, showed the children as evidence, and won the money back.

Lady Anne's two charges would be given education and care but not a life of idleness. They would learn the trade of wife, so that when suitors came along they could offer useful rather than courtly knowledge.

Despite his many and great faults, Lady Anne looked for the best in her husband when he was alive and likewise did so when he was no more. These are her own words, written many years later:

> My first Lord, Richard Sackville, Earl of Dorset, was, in his own nature, of a just mind, of a sweet disposition and very valiant in his own person; he had a great advantage in his breeding, by the wisdom and devotion of his grandfather, Thomas Sackville, who was then one of the wisest men of that time. Though I was happy in many respects being his wife, yet

> was I most unhappy in having the malicious hatred of his brother, then Sir Edward Sackville, toward me, who afterwards came to be Earl of Dorset without heirs male.

Lady Anne was thirteen years married to the earl, who died at thirty-five years and ten days, leaving her a widow aged thirty-four years and two months, with daughters of ten and two years, and the memory of three sons lost. The future was uncertain and was made even more so not two weeks after the earl's death, when first Lady Margaret and then Lady Anne herself went down with the smallpox: '... so extremely and violently that I was at death's door, which infection I took of my eldest child, who had it in great extremity'. There was no knowing how the child would recover and grow but mother could have feared that her face would be martyred by it and she should have no choice but to remain a widow for her life.

Knole became the seat of the new earl and there could be no question of Lady Anne staying there. There was the jointure, which provided a small living and a good house at Bolebroke by Hartfield in Sussex, where the spirit of Anne Boleyn was said to appear on the anniversary of her execution, for it was from this house that Henry VIII courted her. Lady Anne never saw the ghost.

As the dowager countess of Dorset, she also lived at Chenies in Buckinghamshire, which was the principal house of the Russells, her mother's family, and so of the earl of Bedford, before the move was made to Woburn, at which house Lady Anne also stayed for a while.

While at Chenies, the news came first of a war with Spain, after the king had been unable to match Prince Charles with the Infanta, and next of the death of the king himself who had been gravely ill for some time with various afflictions. Unable to hold court, London had been left by him largely to the prince and his machinating close friend, Master Villiers that became Buckingham, and the doings of this pair, once free of King James, did not bode well for a peaceful future. As it came about, the sins of Buckingham caught up with him quite soon after, by which time he was a duke and a most reviled conniver and abuser of the public monies, so that his assassin, who stabbed him, was called hero, which did not save him from the hangman.

King James's death in 1625 meant that one great Solomon was followed by a greater, for King Charles was an even more resolute advocate of the divine right of kings, who failed to see why he needed a parliament when all necessary wisdom was resident within himself. This wisdom would need to be unparalleled in the world, as he sought to unify all corners of the nation in one church under one ruler with no dissent, a task that had been tried before and has since, without notable success.

Such matters did not affect Lady Anne for the present, whose concerns were with herself and her children. There was one piece of excitement, most unlooked for, in May 1626. Her tenants in her Sussex jointure had called in to pay their annual rents, due on the first quarter day being Lady Day, and the last one was collected so there was a deal of money in the house. Late at night, one of the household making a last round outside saw men entering a downstairs chamber through a window. He quickly roused others, who took up swords and confronted the robbers in that chamber, whereupon the miscreants turned and fled.

This was an unusual crime. Common thieves preferred to conduct their business in circumstances that favoured success, and breaking in to the local great house, where men dwelled who could arm themselves, would not conform to their usual run. Lady Anne briefly entertained the thought that her enemy, Sackville, the new earl, was behind it in an attempt, not so much to get the money, but 'to put me to an extreme fright,' but there was no road that could lead to enlightenment on that subject.

Lady Anne's energies now began to be deployed in that necessary dance in noble families, the identification and selection of suitors in marriage of a daughter. Before that could be contemplated, Lady Anne secured her own future—and so her daughters'—by entering a formal claim on her inheritances in Yorkshire and Westmoreland, not to interfere with matters as they lay, as she was forbidden to do, but to make certain there was no possibility of Clifford trickery in years to come.

That settled, Lady Margaret, then aged fourteen, was introduced to John, Lord Tufton, aged twenty-one, and to say that that their attraction was mutual would be an understatement. The wedding was on 21 April 1629; the bride was given away by her cousin, Francis Russell, later the earl of Bedford.

Their first child was born two years after, by which time the groom was the 2nd earl of Thanet, and Lady Margaret would go on to have eleven more children, only two of whom died young.

12

The Countess of Pembroke and Montgomery

At Chenies, the news was a day's hard ride from London, and there Lady Anne heard that King Charles had dissolved parliament amid near riots over certain taxes that the king had levied without consent of the members, and more disturbance over rumours of changes to be made in the church. Nine members had been arrested and sent to the Tower, or some of them have been taken there, and they say that the king would never summon a parliament again. It would seem to most intelligent witnesses, including Lady Anne, that since Queen Elizabeth, monarchs have decreased in sagacity.

During Lady Anne's days at the court of King James, one of the royal favourites had been the greatly handsome Sir Philip Herbert, younger brother of the earl of Pembroke. The Herberts were related to Catherine Parr, last wife of Henry VIII, and Sir Philip's mother was Mary, sister to Sir Philip Sydney, the great man of letters. Letters were not young Herbert's strength, however, he being much more taken with the hawk, the hound, the dice, and the petticoat. It was his skills with the hawk that are supposed to have first brought him to the king's notice, although we may speculate that had he been an ill favoured crookback rather than a beauty, no amount of hawking accomplishments would have brought him to gentleman of the bedchamber and knight of the garter.

So taken was the king that he created Sir Philip earl of Montgomery, and when he was at last displaced in the king's close affections by Lady Anne's old suitor, Robert Kerr, he remained in favour, prospered, did many services for the king, and continued his best loves with a famous zeal, those being hunting of all types of quarry, whether wearing horns or garters, and gambling. By the by, he married to a daughter of the earl of Oxford, Susan de Vere, who bore him children who lived, a girl and three boys, and three more who did not.

This countess of Montgomery, married at the age of seventeen, died at the age of forty-two in 1629. Montgomery himself, already a very wealthy widower, was perhaps soon to become even wealthier as his elder brother, the earl of Pembroke, was in the care of physicians. Montgomery, at forty-five years old was a magnet still for the ladies in his looks and his money, but known to have a violent temper, an arrogant disposition, and an urgent need to seek after every pleasure that could be bought. Later in his life, he would become an important figure in affairs of the state, but for now he looked back rather to the excesses of youth, for the good judgement of maturity had yet to come upon him.

Lady Anne, almost forty years of age, had resolved never to marry again, but the robbery attempt and her suspicions of Edward Sackville and the Cliffords, made her reappraise her situation. Item: not yet an old woman, small of stature, handsome of looks (the smallpox had not had such an effect as Lady Anne saw in her glass). Item: financially independent, and an heiress if an uncertain one. Item: very well connected and of immaculate pedigree.

Looking only for a protector and a life without danger and contrary forces, the ideal match would probably have been a solid, upstanding country gentleman of adequate means and modest habits, who might share his wife's literary interests, who knew the Bible as well as she and followed its teachings, and was without young children of his own and so was not looking for a nursery maid.

> Proverbs XXII i: A good name is rather to be chosen than great riches, and loving favour rather than silver and gold.

Indeed, Lady Anne might have set her own canon of qualities wanting no courtier, for those all were gamblers, cursers, profligates, and men of 'insatiable and gourmand throat' as the scholar Sir Thomas North put it. As matters did come about, Lady Anne could not have created a mightier storm of talk and tattle had she poisoned the queen and married the king nor, as it came about again, could her choice have been more politic.

On 3 June 1630, the widow of six years married, at Chenies, the widower of eighteen months, and she became wife of Philip Herbert, earl of Pembroke (recently inherited) and Montgomery, Lord Chamberlain and knight of the garter, he being one of the greatest subjects in the kingdom and prized beyond most at the court of King Charles. Her younger daughter, Isabella, was present but not her elder daughter, Margaret, who sent word that she prayed God will watch over her mother in this new enterprise.

This was a sentiment felt by all friends of Lady Anne, not one of whom could understand why a person of her character could possibly marry someone like Herbert nor, indeed, why Herbert would want to marry someone like Anne.

> Job XIV vii: For there is hope of a tree, if it be cut down, that it will sprout again, and that the tender branch thereof will not cease.

The country seat of the Herbert family was Wilton House, a grand and ancient mansion near Salisbury in Wiltshire. By November 1630, the family had had a most pleasant summer there, Lady Anne was pregnant, and the way of things in general was well established. For Pembroke, the attractions of London would prove too strong in winter, and the wife would have to make do with her books and her sewing. He was not averse to her going up to court but he would invite her as he chose. When next he returned home, he would bring with him Master Inigo Jones, who would make designs for the restoration and extension of this great house as suggested by the king himself, and the earl would look to his new countess to ensure that works proceeded in good fashion.

So life went on, for four and more years, during which time Lady Anne gave birth to two boys, both arriving too soon and unable to thrive, while she became the earl's amanuensis in the works of whole tribes of building men and craftsmen following the instructions of Master Jones. Contrary to the world's expectations, Lady Anne and the earl were happy for these years, sometimes at Wilton, sometimes at Whitehall, and sometimes together, but the scholar and the libertine do not make the best company *in perpetuo*. The world proved right in the end, and Lady Anne, Bible in hand, agreed to differ with the earl, wagers, purse, and concubine in hand, and beyond their fifth anniversary hardly saw each other, except when the earl gave support in her legal claims, registering her rights to her lands again in case of a Clifford stroke. Still often at Wilton, Lady Anne also stayed at Baynard's Castle, a very ancient place by the city wall, where Richard III once lived, and Edward IV was proclaimed king (the building perished in the Great Fire of 1666).

In 1633, a lawyer, William Prynne, had parts of his ears cut off for publishing a volley of words against plays and masques, as immoral and contrary to the will of God. Such pamphlets were not rare, as those severe folk calling themselves Puritans constantly tried to take all to a life of work and prayer and nothing else. Lady Anne spent much of her own time in work and prayer, but she knew that all work can lead to as much misery in its own way, as all play. Master Prynne's pamphlet was especially noticed because he applied the term 'whore' to any woman who appeared in plays and entertainments, which would nominate Lady Anne, for her parts in those masques of long ago, but more drastically for Pryne it seemed to have the queen as target, who had given a part in a play at court during Christmas last, which festival also is damned by the Puritans as heathen. As he likewise attacked those who watched plays, that was taken as a direct reference to the king. Before the Star Chamber, he was fined £5,000, sent to the Tower and told he must have his ears cropped.

It was about this time that feelings began to run through the country that King Charles was embarked on a secret journey back towards papistry. His queen was a Roman Catholic, and he had welcomed various papal envoys. The imposition by Archbishop Laud of the new prayer book in Scotland caused great commotion, and the Scots had never wanted the bishops. As might have been foretold, such matters, while there was no parliament, were the beginnings of the worst disaster ever to befall the nation.

In 1635, Pembroke made over to Lady Anne her jointure of those lands of his in the Isle of Sheppey that were formerly the jointure of his first wife. He also released his right to all her lands in Westmoreland and those lands in Craven that were a part of Lady Isabella's portion, if ever those lands should fall to her in life.

In 1637, poor Master Prynne was been under the knife again, for his continued attacks on the works of Archbishop Laud, which, under direction of the king, were seen by some as a progress back to the Old Religion. Although he was in the Tower, he wrote his addresses and had them secretly taken and printed. He was again before the Star Chamber and sentenced to be pilloried, to have the remainder of his ears cut off, his nose slit, and to be branded on his face, and to stay in prison until he died.

> Romans XII xix: Dearly beloved, avenge not yourselves, but rather give place unto wrath: for it is written, Vengeance is mine; I will repay, saith the Lord.

While Puritans such as Prynne were pulling in one direction, the king pulled in the other and decided that it was time the Scots, once ruled as a separate nation by his father, King James, should be brought firmly under control. The result was the opposite of that intended and a near independence of the Scots, many of whom signed a covenant that they would defend the Presbyterian religion to the death. They saw themselves warranted by God to defeat papistry, by which they meant anything not of the presbytery, such as stained glass windows, the surplice, stone altars, kneeling to pray and more. There would be a Scottish parliament, whatever the king might say, and so an English army was assembled and marched north to quell the rebels, in command of the king himself.

When the Scottish Army was sighted at Duns, the king knew he could not win with his ill-made rabble and so signed a treaty at Berwick that allowed the Scots to pass laws. Acts of the Scottish parliament still required the king's approval, and when their acts were passed, the king refused to approve them.

On the point of losing Scotland and in the severest financial difficulties, King Charles recalled parliament in London as a desperate throw. Instead of taking heed of the king's instruction and granting monies to the crown, parliament debated the many grievances of the people and would not allow taxes or subsidies until peace was made with the Scots. In a fury, the king dissolved parliament again, which had sat for barely three weeks and so became known as the Short Parliament.

Popery and the Divine Right of Kings were thought by many to be an alliance made in hell, planned to subdue and trample the free English citizen. By citizen was meant only such as can be voted to parliament and could vote for such, which were men of substance, the knights of the shires and the property owners in the boroughs. This freedom from trampling was not meant for the man who toiled in the fields, nor the smith in his rented shop nor, indeed, any woman whatsoever.

On the other side was the king, who would not listen to parliament's demands that would raise their power and diminish the monarch's. King Charles was truly convinced that unless he scattered the Scots to the four winds, especially those called Covenanters, the Church of England would be taken over by theirs and so he must move closer to the Pope for protection.

This served only to make the Puritans ever more against the king, and ever more pure so that they would have every pleasure forbidden for all, and all women bound to the house or other labours, denied any books that might promote thought, and stepping forth only if veiled like, so folk heard, the Mahometan women and the Hindus.

The Scots invaded England, defeated the English Army, and occupied Newcastle and Durham. A treaty allowed them to stay there, paid for by King Charles, until a full and lasting peace could be negotiated, for which purpose an English parliament was summoned again. This parliament, the king agreed, could not be dissolved without its own consent and from that moment on, everything King Charles did or tried to do only added to his own discredit.

He recalled the earl of Strafford from Ireland, where he had been governor, promising no harm could come to him, and soon after signed his death warrant. The king of England went to Scotland and tried to raise an army to subdue England, and he entered the House of Commons with soldiers to arrest some of the members. Such a thing had never been done, with or without soldiers; the plan had been betrayed so the birds had flown before arresting.

In the meantime, not to forget Lady Anne's fortunes in these terrible times, in January 1641, her uncle, Cumberland, died, aged eighty-one, at Skipton castle, with title and disputed estates passing to her cousin, Henry Clifford, who had no male heirs but was like to live as long as his late brother. In May, her friend and constant adviser and supporter, Francis Russell, earl of Bedford, died.

On 10 January 1642, a few days after his disastrous entry to the House of Commons, King Charles left London to gather forces about him and prepare for war. The nation began to divide, on the one hand the Royalists, who believed in the way things had been and hated the Puritans; on the other, those who feared a return to papism and who wanted less power for the king and more for parliament. This is a simplification of the quarrel, and there were many more matters consistent and not. It might have been expected that the great families would have been all for the king. Not so, for the earls of Manchester, Warwick, and Essex, and many other nobles, were for parliament, who possessed great wealth and influence. The king depended entirely on others for money to pay and feed his soldiers, such as the earls of Newcastle and Derby.

Lady Anne was for the king, while her husband, lately removed from his post of Lord Chancellor by King Charles, had decided for parliament although moderately so. For most of the year of 1642, they stayed at Wilton, and were there when the king raised his standard at Nottingham, on 22 August.

By the October, the war had grown hotter and hotter. Knole was seized by parliament and many valuables stolen, and the threat remained of more such from either side looking for gold to pay the fight. Pembroke, Lady Anne, and her daughter, Isabella, left Wilton for London, he to his lodgings at the Cockpit in St James's Park to be near the parliament, while daughter and mother stayed at Baynard's, which was a house full of riches. They prayed that they and the riches remained secure.

The king had moved to a temporary base near Shrewsbury and now decided to leave there to march on London. He had a large army but not much of it was experienced or professional, so when they happened to come across the parliament army at Edge Hill, in Warwickshire, the result was a shambles. Parliament forces under the earl of Essex were also a long way from fighting efficiency and the battle, which had had the potential for ending the war before it really began, was inconclusive. Prince Rupert and the royalist cavalry were superior to parliament's undrilled horsemen. While some of the king's foot soldiers were 'gentlemen's sons and persons of quality', as Oliver Cromwell put it, many had no weapons at all, while parliament's men, unfit though they were, did have better equipment. Many men died and each side claimed a mortal wound on the other, though the king had the better claim to victory and carried on with his march on London.

> Isiah II iv: And he shall judge among the nations, and shall rebuke many people: and they shall beat their swords into plowshares, and their spears into pruning hooks: nation shall not lift up sword against nation, neither shall they learn war any more.

King Charles was stopped by the earl of Essex with a greater force at Turnham Green and had to retire to Reading. And so began the real struggle, which saw the royalists gain at first, but parliament turn the tide towards the end of 1643; Lady Anne was at Baynard's the while. She, daughter of the great Clifford, twice a countess, had her forming years at the court of Queen Elizabeth and, being of that age before the gold in the crown was worn so thin, stayed a loyal royalist, which would have become dangerous for her without Pembroke's protection. Her husband was no soldier but a politician, and he was sent by parliament to negotiate with the king, and in this way was able to stay always on the best side to be, and his power to shield his wife, estranged though she was from him, became a principal matter at the end of that year.

In December, Henry Clifford died at York. He had a daughter living, Lady Elizabeth Clifford, who had married the earl of Cork and they had children, including sons, but they were not part of the king's award nor of George Clifford's original will, and so, at last, the lands were Lady Anne's, yet they were not because she could not go there.

Skipton castle stood for the king, having been garrisoned by her cousin, Clifford, and had been besieged by parliament's men for a year or more. Appleby castle likewise was garrisoned for the king and beset by a great toing and froing, with Scottish soldiers everywhere and no clear view from London of what was happening. Should parliament prevail, as her husband Pembroke said it surely would, then in what state would these places be, and how should they be Lady Anne's if they were the spoils of war?

Her daughter, Isabella, had passed her twenty-first birthday on 6 October, which had brought her more to Pembroke's notice than on other days. It was the cause of a great anger and falling out between him and his wife as he called Isabella an old maid, and said she should wed with his youngest son, James Herbert, while she still could.

Pembroke's oldest son had been wed at fifteen but was dead of the smallpox; the middle son was also married; leaving this James, who was of an age with Isabella but was an ancient scholar in spirit and suitable for a lawyer.

Now that the Yorkshire and Westmoreland estates were his wife's, in name if not in possession, Isabella's portion, which was £5,000, made her an additional attraction to my lord. The elder of the living sons, Philip, would inherit the titles and estates of Pembroke and Montgomery, and so the father saw an opportunity to make the Clifford lands a dowry for James.

Lady Isabella was most averse to the match, a matter that Pembroke saw as unimportant and demanded that his wife change her mind for her. She could not and would not do so, so there were two determined women in Pembroke's way, howsoever he raged, raging being an aspect of his character in which he surpassed all. Lady Anne's first lord was the father, and with no father in the business, the daughter would choose for herself. Lady Isabella did have a secret love who was, as the Scots say, a braw gallant, called James Compton, and he fought for the king, and so the ladies would have to wait to see what might come of it. This secret love would be a hazard indeed if parliament were to prevail, and the year had ended with two victories for that side.

Earlier, in March, there had been a cavalry skirmish in Shropshire at Hopton Heath. The royalist commander, the earl of Northampton—Lord Spencer Compton, a constant companion of Dorset—was unhorsed but fought on, cursing the base rogues and rebels who then killed him. Though the fight was no great decider either way, the death of the earl was deemed a victory in itself.

His heir, James Compton, at Hopton Heath with his father, thus became earl and a cavalry commander with Prince Rupert at the Battle of Newbury where, despite charge after charge, the parliament foot held against the royalist horse and forced a withdrawal.

This James, earl of Northampton, was but a few weeks older than the maid Isabella and was much more to her fancy than the safe but dry James that Pembroke would have her wed. Despite the dangers, mother and daughter agreed that love was worth a wait.

There was business to attend, as well as affairs of the heart. It was the law that a tenancy of land ended when the landlord died, and the tenant had to reapply if he wished to stay on that land, and pay a sum for the privilege. It came to Lady Anne's notice that King Charles had superseded her at Skipton, and had had agents gathering rents and charges as if he were the new landlord after Clifford, and was paying his garrison with the money so collected. A messenger was sent quietly to Sir John Lowther, to ensure that the Westmoreland tenants paid nothing to anyone until such time as Lady Anne herself could decide on their cases. Sir John was well placed for this duty, he being appointed by the king as governor of Brougham castle and commissioner of array for the county, which is to say he was given the further duty of raising troops for the royal cause. He had lately been member of parliament for Westmoreland and, though officially a colonel in the royal army, was careful never to go into actual danger for the cause.

In July 1644 came the greatest battle so far, indeed the first complete trial of all the forces, and at Marston Moor in Yorkshire, the royalists went to utter defeat and gave up the north entirely to parliament. Skipton castle still stood out but could not influence the war nor hope for anything more than it had: surrender at Christmas 1645 and the castle wrecked inside.

Over the next months, all the royalist strongholds fell or ceased to be of concern, and the power of the army, under Oliver Cromwell, began to exceed that of the parliament that had given it birth. The king gave up himself to the Scots in May 1646; Lady Anne's husband, the earl of

Pembroke, took with him other parliament men and various proposals for peace, which were a list of concessions and promises for the king to accept or not, two answers that proved too decisive for the king. Though defeated in the field, the other parties vying for power saw the king as the key to their own supremacy and the king knew this, and so by turn he was passed from Scottish custody, to parliament's, to the army's, while the king courted a match with each.

Matters were not resolved and patience was lost, so that the king himself was arrested, on 3 June 1647, on Cromwell's orders from the place where he had been secured by Pembroke. The puritan and Presbyterian factions of parliament combined with the Scots and the royalists and set out to begin another war against the army that had just won the previous one.

James Compton, earl of Northampton, was one of the many royalist commanders who had given his parole not to take up arms again for the king, and was one of the smaller number who kept his word. He and Isabella were married on 16 July 1647 without Lady Anne in attendance, giving 'for many reasons' as the clearest explanation at offer. Needless to say, Pembroke was not present either, and we can surmise that the whole business was conducted in as much secrecy as could be, given that a royalist earl married a royalist countess's daughter while the centre of the royalist cause, the king, was held prisoner at Hampton Court, and the army occupied London and ruled parliament.

The newlyweds were to live at a house in Canonbury, it being too hazardous to go to Castle Ashby, the great mansion in Northamptonshire that was sacked by the parliament soldiers in the war, or to the older house where Queen Elizabeth, King James, and King Charles had all been guests, Compton Wynyates in Warwickshire. That had also been sacked with much booty taken. The earl and the new countess would have to live the quiet life until order returned to the world. There was a fire at Wilton, cause unknown, damage difficult to assess. Inigo Jones went back there to sort things out and rebuild as necessary.

Cromwell's version of order was becoming clear, as he came into London with, some say, 20,000 men, took possession of the Tower and established himself at what was called Head Quarters, in Putney, Surrey. Here there were debates about the future of the kingdom, which included such radical proposals as one-man-one-vote and power to be vested in the House of Commons.

In November 1647, the fat was truly spilled on the fire. The king escaped his captors and ran to the Isle of Wight, to Carisbrooke, from where he sent yet another set of terms and matters to be treated, which only served to exasperate the opposing parties. At the same time, there were secret encouragements to the Scots to invade England again and save it for the Stuart line, but parliament spies knew all and there would be no more treating with the king. Parliament would act as necessary without the king. They would stop short of the *res publica* of old Rome but would keep the king to one side.

In 1648, the war blew up again and royalist flags were waved in many parts, but only in far Wales, Essex, and the north did this new rebellion last. The castles at Pontefract and Scarborough were under siege, but Appleby surrendered to the Scots in July. Royalist and Scots forces were not in coordination and Cromwell dealt them a fatal blow at Preston Moor. Thus was the second war ended, with much revenge taken against those who had led the royalists. Skipton castle was pulled down almost to the foundations; the Appleby Scots surrendered and the castle was much reduced. Now there was nothing left of the royalist cause, save for the cause of it, and that was nullified in January 1649.

The king was tried for treason in a court without judges, for none would sit in judgement there, and Pembroke would have no part of it. On the day of his execution, a great number of soldiers kept between the scaffold and the crowd, so that the common people and others there could not hear what the king said. Certain persons close by did hear, and the king, noble and in dignity to the end, declared that the sovereign and a subject are clean different things, and that liberty of the people consists in having government, of which they should have no share. Whatsoever his faults as a government, he died in his faith and as a true Christian. It was done on Lady Anne's fifty-ninth birthday, 30 January 1649.

Lady Anne was feeling alone again. Her marriage was by now in name only, her blessed daughters were wed and happy, and London had entirely lost its charms. She decided she would journey to the wild lands as soon as she could and never return.

> 2 Samuel XXII xxxi & xxx: For thou art my lamp, O Lord, and the Lord will lighten my darkness. For by thee I have run through a troop: by my God have I leapt over a wall.

Now were there earthquakes in parliament, but when the dust settled, there was at least a certain stability in England. Six weeks or so after the king's head was cut off, parliament abolished the monarchy altogether, and the House of Lords, and later proclaimed the country a Commonwealth, and about two weeks after that, Lady Anne took her final leave of her husband on 3 June 1649. On that Sunday, she took her leave of her second lord at his lodgings at the Cockpit. He kissed her and she him. He wished her well and she him. He knew what her intentions were—to restore the estates and order them—and they could neither of them see any place for him in that enterprise.

She went first to her daughter Northampton's house in Islington, which was the first time she was ever in any of that lord's houses and she fancied it would be the last. The elder daughter, Margaret, countess of Thanet, had no great house of her own, for her lord had been much reduced by parliament for his part in the war, when he fought for the king. One house, Bodlam castle in Sussex, he had to sell for the fines levied upon him by the new government, and other houses and estates had been taken as punishment. They hoped to settle in Hothfield, in Kent, although there was no suitable house there.

There were nine grandchildren, five sons living and four daughters. The one who died was Lady Anne Tufton, named for grandmother. There would be another Lady Anne Tufton, who would live, and visits to the north by numbers of Tuftons and Northamptons would be a great joy in later years. She gave them all presents and said her farewells with tears and smiles, hoping and praying this would not be like her own leaving of her mother, never to see daughter again.

> Psalms CXXVII vii: Our soul is escaped as a bird out of the snare of the fowlers: the snare is broken, and we are escaped.

Lady Anne had no ready money and so approached her friend, the dowager countess of Kent, Lady Elizabeth Talbot, to lend her £100. In paying it back soon afterwards, Lady Anne wrote:

> Your goodness and noble kindness has been so great and constant to me for so many years together, as that there is now no creature alive, man or woman, to whom I am so much obliged as to your worthy self, therefore do me the right to believe, I am, Madam, your Ladyship's cousin and most true, humble servant.

After so many years of trials and sufferings, the day of destiny came and Lady Anne set forth from London on 11 July 1649, nearly forty-four years since her father died and left the estates elsewhere. But what was she coming to, Lady Anne, after a lifetime of—mostly—comfort, high society, kings and queens, and large households? The earl of Pembroke had a household staff of eighty at his London house and another 100-plus at Wilton; Lady Anne would make do with rather fewer.

Westmoreland life at that time, though not as bleak and tough as in the lake-land fells of Cumberland, was still a long way behind Southern England. In the kinder climes of the Eden valley, where all Lady Anne's castles were, at least there were good prospects for growing wheat and barley and raising cattle, whereas Cumberland could mostly offer only oats and their specially hardy sheep that gave one lamb per ewe and never a decent fatty joint of mutton, only dry muscle.

Improvements in plough design had yet to come in, and the usual cultivation method was the wooden plough that merely scratched the soil rather than turned it over, drawn by four oxen. No root crops were grown for fodder so farmers had no means of keeping all their animals over the winter. The autumnal slaughter was a festive occasion followed by much pickling and salting, to preserve every bit of meat.

This was how it had been for centuries, in the pre-industrial, backward north, where every sniff at soft southerners was well justified, if envious.

There was also trouble brewing among the tenants. No rents had been paid for five years or more, with no agent to collect them, and Lady Anne had no secretaries, stewards, or other employees with knowledge and experience of the estates. Boundaries had been secretly moved to suit local arguments, no manorial courts had been held, and the imposition of order was bound to be difficult and fractious.

There was more trouble still between Lady Anne and her cousin, Elizabeth, daughter of Henry, the last earl of Cumberland, and now the countess of Cork. The land surrounding Barden Tower, the old hunting lodge made into a fine house by the Shepherd Lord, Henry Clifford, but decayed by this time to a ruin, bordered with the earl of Cork's estates at Bolton Abbey, and Elizabeth thought that land should be hers, by inheritance from her father. Lady Anne disagreed and, after discussion, matters were resolved in her favour without recourse to outside adjudication.

Lady Anne's plan was to go first to Skipton, where she arrived on the 18th to see the dreadful damage wrought by the parliament's men on her place of birth. There was a visit to Barden Tower, and in August, the new mistress of the north removed to her most ancient seat, Appleby castle, and visited Brougham also, forty-two years since seeing either.

Ecclesiastes III i & v: To every thing there is a season, and a time to every purpose under the heaven. A time to cast away stones, and a time to gather stones together.

Over the next weeks, Lady Anne saw Brough castle and the remains of Pendragon, and she began to lay her plans for restoring everything that could be restored. This was a perilous matter that could be seen as a defiance of parliament and, in particular, a defiance of Cromwell. When her friends in the north counselled against such action, urging delay until peace was confirmed everywhere, Lady Anne answered in her own fashion.

'Let Master Cromwell destroy my castles if he will, and as often as he levels them, I will rebuild them, so long as I have credit or he leaves a shilling in my pocket.' This little speech reached Cromwell's ears and his response was surprising, perhaps coming out of a certain respect for such a resilient and determined woman. 'Nay,' he said, 'Let her build what she will. She shall have no hindrance from me.'

Still staying at Appleby castle, news came to her there on 27 January 1650 that her husband, Philip Herbert, had died in his lodgings in London on the 23rd. His body was to be buried beside his brother and their father and mother in Salisbury Cathedral. Lady Anne's second lord was no scholar at all to speak of, for he was not past three or four months at the University of Oxford, being taken away from there presently after his father's death in Queen Elizabeth's time. It was decided that he should follow the court, being fittest for that kind of life, when he was about sixteen years old. No academic maybe, but he had a very quick apprehension, a sharp understanding, very shrewd, and of a discerning spirit, which was how he came to hold the office of Lord Chamberlain to the king for so many years. His wife and friends saw another side to his nature, being extremely choleric.

Job VIII ix: For we are but of yesterday, and know nothing, because our days upon earth are a shadow.

Lady Anne was now sixty years of age and gaining new strength every day from her victory in freedom. There had been an excellent tutor for this, as she remembered herself as a youth under the guiding hand of Queen Elizabeth, and no better model could there have been upon which to fashion her policies, for Lady Anne was queen, and all in Westmoreland and Craven were her subjects.

Some of those subjects were in rebellious mood, having been neglected for years, their grievances not examined and only one side of their tenancy agreements, the payment side, being enacted. There were examples of hardship, but there were also attempts to take advantage of Lady Anne's newness and unfamiliarity. Once more, the lawyers had to be recruited.

Shortly after Pembroke's death, Lady Anne removed to Skipton (13 February), stopping off at the Kirkby Lonsdale inn for one night (probably the inn now known as the Sun), a route that then took her over the dales via Ingleton, Clapham, and Settle. It was, obviously, the first time she had been back to her birthplace.

> At this time of my staying there I enjoyed myself in building and reparations at Skipton and Bardon Tower, and in causing the boundaries to be ridden, and my houses kept in my several manners in Craven, and in those kind of country affairs about my estate. Which I found in extreme disorder by reason it had been so long kept from me, from the death of my father until this time, and by occasion of the late civil wars in England, and in this time the suits and differences in law began to grow hot between my tenants in Westmoreland and some of my tenants in Craven and me. And while I now abode there, was my eldest daughter the Countess of Thanet delivered of her son George Tufton at Hothfield House in Kent, I accounting it a great blessing to have a grandchild of mine to bear my noble father's name.

Through the 1630s and '40s, Lady Margaret had borne her husband ten children, only one of whom died young, and of the five sons until now, four would become earls of Thanet in succession as elder brothers died. George was the last boy, and died before reaching maturity; one more daughter, Anne, came in 1654, and that was the end of child-bearing for Lady Margaret.

Christmas 1650 was spent at Skipton castle, a most happy one with Lady Anne's eldest grandchild, Nicholas Lord Tufton, there with her. He was nineteen years old and a very model of a noble lord. When he left, he would return to London and go on beyond the sea to travel to Italy and other places, and he would succeed to the earldom in 1664.

During that Christmas, Lady Anne purchased a parcel of land below Appleby castle, at the top of Boroughgate, which was to be her hospital of Saint Anne, thirteen alms houses for widows who were too old or infirm to work, where they would live without rent and be sustained by an allowance.

Other building work had strange benefits indeed. The war broke out again, with royalist forces in Scotland under the young Charles II, and a parliamentary garrison occupied the newly repaired Appleby castle commanded by Major-General Thomas Harrison, one of those who signed the warrant for the execution of King Charles. His soldiers filled the castle, the town, and many further parts, and a strong cavalry force sought to stop the royalists, although according to Lady Anne 'the King and his army that August came into England and within six or seven miles of Appleby castle'.

General Harrison accused Lady Anne of sending help to the young king who was coming south with his Scottish army, and demanded to know of her opinion, when she slept and lived but at his mercy. She replied that she could not help the king but she loved him, and would live and die in her loyalty, and there was the truth for the general to act upon as he would.

At one point, the young king was at Kendal and some of his Scottish army at Penrith, and all expected a siege at Appleby. Instead, they went past and marched south, and the general and his men soon went also.

The upshot was a great battle at Worcester in September 1651, and the royalists were defeated by Cromwell. Charles was not taken, for which Lady Anne praised God, for surely the government would see an invasion of England by Scots as treason and give out the same fate to the son as befell his father.

All the while, far away from politics, Lady Anne became more and more enamoured of the rural existence:

> And in this settled abode of mine in these three ancient houses of mine inheritance, Appleby castle and Brougham castle in Westmoreland, and Skipton castle in Craven, I do more and more fall in love with the contentments and innocent pleasures of a country life. Which humour of mine I do wish with all my heart (if it be the will of almighty God) may be conferred on my posterity that are to succeed me in these places, for a wife and lady oneself, to make their own houses the place of self-fruition and be comfortably part of this life.
>
> But this must be left to a succeeding providence, for none can know what shall come after them. Ecclesiastes III xxii: Wherefore I perceive that there is nothing better, than that a man should rejoice in his own works; for that is his portion: for who shall bring him to see what shall be after him?

> But to invite them to it that saying in Psalm XVI may be fittingly applied: 'The lot is fallen unto me in a pleasant place. I have a fair heritage'. And I may truly say that here 'From many noble progenitors I hold transmitted lands, castles and honours which they sway'd of old'.
>
> All of which benefits have been bestowed upon me for the heavenly goodness of my dear mother, whose fervent prayers were offered up with greater zeal to almighty God for me and mine, and had such return of blessings followed them, as that though I met with some bitter and wicked enemies and many great oppositions in this world, yet were my delieverance so great, as would not befall to any who were not visibly sustained by a divine favour from above.
>
> And in this country life of mine I find also that saying of the psalmist true: 'The earth is full of the goodness of the Lord'.

Lady Anne set about her building works and spent many thousands of pounds on restoring five castles as residences if not as fortresses, seven churches, and the tower of Barden, and various new works such as the bridge, the grammar school, and the alms-houses at Appleby. Here was much paid work provided for the men of those districts, and Lady Anne was at pains to see and be seen, as she rode the bounds and travelled between far places, often over the roughest ground.

Every Monday after breakfast, a small sort of court was held, when money was given to twenty poor people, and her kitchen folk were instructed never to turn away a hungry person. There were cases at law with certain tenants, one of which proved so intractable and beyond the lawyers' abilities to resolve that Oliver Cromwell, now the self-proclaimed protector, offered to intervene to decide it, as King James had done all those years before. When Cromwell's emissaries came to Appleby, Lady Anne's response was the same as it had been then: 'I shall never refer any of my concerns in that kind to the Protector nor any person living, but leave it wholly to the direction of the law. I refused to submit to King James on the like account and will do likewise to the Protector, whatsoever hazard or danger is incurred thereby'.

There was much travel, especially between Appleby and Skipton, and much visiting by grandchildren. John Tufton, second grandson, came to stay for almost a whole year, before going to 'Eton College there to study for some time and to live as a scholar', and afterwards to Queens College, Oxford.

In 1652, an old enemy died, Edward Sackville, younger brother of Lady Anne's first husband and earl of Dorset, so she had outlasted him as well, and her daughter Margaret, countess of Thanet, gave birth to her eleventh child, a girl called Mary. The following January, Lady Anne passed an important year, according to the old philosophers. This was her climacteric, her sixty-third birthday, when she was supposedly at greater risk of disaster—or death—than in other years that were not multiples of seven (seven years old being the first climacteric).

The Appleby alms-houses were finished at last, after five years in the building, and a full set of tenants installed, being 'twelve good women, eleven widows and one injured maid', including one who had a child with her from her marriage to a minister, now deceased.

Her daughter, Isabella, gave birth to William, her second son. He, like so many, would not live long. The father, James Compton, earl of Northampton, visited Lady Anne and saw around the Westmoreland and Craven estates, and there was another wedding, Lady Anne's granddaughter, Margaret Tufton, to George, Baron Coventry, whose father had been an important figure on the royalist side in the Civil War.

In September, there was great celebration when Margaret, with her husband, the earl of Thanet, and eldest son, Nicholas, made the journey from London, over Stainmore to Appleby, and stayed at the castle for eleven nights. This was the first time that either of Lady Anne's children had visited their mother's inheritance, the story of which must have dominated their early lives. They returned by the Lancashire route through Worcester, to stay with the new Lady Coventry at the family house in Croome.

At the end of the year (1653), Lady Anne moved to Brougham castle, which had fallen into disrepair since she left it in 1616 to get married, and King James was there in 1617. Now habitable, after much work and expense, Lady Anne could take as her chamber the room where her father was born and her mother died.

More births came in 1654, with Margaret having Anne, her twelfth child at the age of forty, and granddaughter Margaret Coventry producing a son, John, which made Lady Anne a great-grandmother for the first time. Not all news was happy; Lady Anne's first grandson, Nicholas Tufton, was sent to the Tower by Cromwell on suspicion of being involved in a royalist plot, and another grandchild, Lady Frances Tufton, had to be taken abroad, to Utrecht, where she was promised a cure for her rickets, 'which she had in great extremity'.

A journey north was still a mighty undertaking, and in 1656, Margaret Thanet brought with her in her coach three of her young children—Cecily aged eight, George six, and Mary four. There were servants in attendance of course, but what an adventure this must have seemed to those little ones who had only known London, travelling days on terrible roads to arrive at the forbidding walls of Brougham castle.

In that same year, granddaughter Margaret Coventry had a daughter who died the next day, and daughter Isabella Northampton had her fourth child, a daughter, who would die a year later. Looking forward to her own death, Lady Anne had the work completed on her tomb in Appleby church, part of that project being repairs to the main body of the church, which cost her several hundred pounds.

At Skipton, a most curious incident occurred. A fellow of Halifax, a rich merchant in the cloth trade called Murgatroyd, purchased a tenancy and proposed to live thereon in the manner of a gentleman. As had been the case for centuries, a part of ordinary rents was in kind—parcels of oats or other grain or, often, fowls. In addition to his money, this Murgatroyd was to pay one hen, which he refused to do.

If Lady Anne were to ignore this transgression, then all the other tenants would do the same, which would be the loss of many hundreds of hens in Westmoreland and Yorkshire, 800 at Appleby alone, used to feed her several households, which, though modest, could not afford such a loss.

She took Master Murgatroyd to court, to the York assizes, at the considerable expense of £200, and won the case, whereupon an invitation was issued to said Murgatroyd to dine with his landlady at Skipton castle. He came, and was dining, when she informed him that the fowl he was eating was the very one he had paid in rent.

At this time, the worship of God was dictated by new puritanical laws that forbade the use of the Book of Common Prayer and all the rites and services of the Church of England as Lady Anne and everyone had been used to practise and which had been set out in the laws of Queen Elizabeth, although one was kept, which was for all to attend church once a week or be fined a shilling. The punishment for one of Lady Anne's standing and property, should the new law be disobeyed, would be sequestration, which is to say her estates and incomes would become the government's, and herself would be excommunicated from what we might call Cromwell's church.

Lady Anne's answer was to maintain a chaplain at each of her main residences, being the castles of Skipton, Appleby, and Brougham, and to hold the weekly services of the Church of England in her private chapels. Parliament threatened sequestration, but Lady Anne ignored it, and the threat was never carried out.

When Cromwell died in 1658, the lord protectorship passed to his son, Richard, for all the world as if a king had died, but he did not last long as he had no support in the army. A small matter of vandalism committed by that army in 1648 was repeated ten years on, when person or persons unknown ripped down the second of two famous horns from an oak tree. The story goes back to 1333, when Edward Balliol, king of Scotland, was hunting in Whinfield Park in the company of Robert Clifford, staying at Appleby or Brougham. They killed a great stag and nailed its horns to a nearby oak tree and over the years those horns grew into the wood and became the local legend of the Hartshorn Tree. As Lady Anne wrote: 'Whereby we may see that Time brings to forgetfulness any memorable thing in this world, be they never so carefully preserved'.

Rumblings of royalists and presbyterians turned into an uprising but too soon, and some of the conspirators, among them James Compton, earl of Northampton, were put in the Tower, and there Northampton stayed for a few months with his wife, too, Lady Anne's second daughter, Isabella, who produced their third son and fifth child in April 1659, called James. Although this was 'the first time that she had two sons alive at one time', as Lady Anne put it, the new boy was not to have anything but a very short life, dying three years later. The same fate befell Thomas Coventry, new son of Lady Anne's granddaughter, Margaret.

Parliament, seemingly expecting trouble in the north, garrisoned soldiers at Appleby and Skipton, also Brougham. Nicholas, Lord Tufton, went on a secret mission to France in aid of King Charles, but matters came to a head when General Monck, lately Cromwell's commander-in-chief, invaded England from Scotland and occupied London on 3 February 1660. The new parliament, sitting in April, with members from Westmoreland including Lady Anne's cousins, Sir Thomas Wharton and Sir John Lowther, cleared the way for the king's return and he made his triumphant entry to the City of London, on 29 May.

The celebrations were mighty in Appleby, that town where no man could be found to declare the proscription of the young prince as a traitor, and so they had to get one from Kirkby Stephen.

In 1660, Lady Anne was seventy-one years old but of a sudden felt like a girl again, for the king was restored and the church likewise. She put aside her customary garb of black serge and with her two gentlewomen went through her several trunks of things from days gone to find a gown more suitable for a great occasion. Neither of the gentlewomen suggested that the old gowns might not fit, which was as well because they all did and so they only had to choose which one. They settled on the sea-green silk of long ago, in the time of Lord Dorset, and for the while she could be her gentlewomen's equal in dress.

They went into Appleby town and the church of Saint Lawrence, where was buried her blessed mother and where she too would rest when her time came, and after a joyous service they processed up the street of Boroughgate, where there were bonfires amain and crowds of folk cheering, with the mayor, the aldermen and all the gentlemen and ladies of the district, to a high platform dressed in tapestries and cloth of gold, which they ascended to the sound of many trumpets. They knelt before a crown, and the king was proclaimed, and they prayed for him and drank his health, still on their knees, though the mayor said Lady Anne should sit but she told him she would kneel among all.

All were welcome after at the castle and there was a great feasting there, and at Brougham and at Skipton where she had ordered something similar to mark this glorious day when their king and their church were returned to them.

The new king granted open pardon to all who had taken up arms against him and his father and was anxious to reinstate a proper parliament rather than one selected by Cromwell and the army. The exceptions were those men who had signed the death warrant of King Charles, and among them was Thomas Harrison, who had confronted Lady Anne at Appleby castle, and he was hanged, drawn, and quartered at Charing Cross.

So life and death continued. Children and grandchildren made the journey north to see the great lady, quite frequently considering the distance and the effort it took, which was a great joy to her but often short-lived. Lady Isabella Northampton came with her two eldest, Lord William and Lady Anne, to stay at Barden Tower in July and August 1660, and they said their goodbyes on the 6th. One year later, both children were dead, which was likewise the last time that Lady Anne saw her daughter, who bore a daughter, Alethea, in 1661 but herself died later that year aged thirty-nine.

Repairs continued to castles and churches, great-grandchildren were born to live long or, alas, to die young, justice was administered, charity was given, Lady Anne and her retinue removed regularly between Skipton, Appleby, and Brougham, business was conducted, harvests were gathered in. Old friends and cousins died far away in London, but she was never tempted to make a journey to Court to meet the king. The life here, with its seasonal rounds, its news and its small matters, kept her content for many more years.

Repairs to Brough castle in 1661 meant Lady Anne could go and stay there and supervise the old mill being pulled down and rebuilt.

> I now lay [at Brough] for three nights together, the first night in that half round tower called Clifford's Tower, and the other two nights in the second room of the great tower called Roman Tower, both of which towers and castle were newly repaired by me to my exceeding great cost and charges after they had layen desolate ever since the timber thereof was casually burned in the year 1521. [On the] fourteenth day of October did I remove out of Appleby castle into Pendragon castle since it was lately repaired and made habitable by me to my great costs and charges after it had layen desolate ever since the fifteenth year of Edward the Third in 1341, which is 320 years ago, for then the Scots made an inroad into the West if England totally destroying it and pulling down all the timber and a great part of the stone building of it..

Lady Anne's granddaughter, Lady Margaret Coventry, gave birth to her fifth child, a boy, who died a few days later, and her much favoured grandson, William, Lord Compton, died aged eight at the Northampton country seat, Castle Ashby, which had been so looted and knocked about by the parliamentary army. Even worse news arrived to say that her daughter, Lady Isabella, had died on the same day as the Pendragon move, 14 October, at Northampton House, Lincoln's Inn Fields, leaving only two children left alive, James aged two and newly born Alethea. Their father would wed again and children from that marriage would live to inherit the titles and estates. Young James died at three, it would seem of cancerous growths in his lungs; Alethea was eighteen when she died.

Lady Anne's health remained mainly robust, although she had a scare on 22 March 1662, when she had 'a swounding fit whereby I was in great danger of death, but it pleased God to restore me to life and health again in a very short space'. Still there was no temptation to make the journey south, even though the new Queen Catherine of Braganza, Infanta of Portugal, had arrived in England to marry King Charles II, and the king's mother, Queen Marie, also came back to England. Lady Margaret went to see Queen Catherine at Hampton Court while Lady Anne stayed in Brough. Catherine was a Roman Catholic, and her faith would cause a certain amount of trouble during her married life. She produced no children alive, while husband Charles fathered many among his various mistresses.

In the Clifford years, before Lady Anne took over and even before the chaos caused by the Civil War, the landlords of Westmoreland had been largely absentee and often unsympathetic to their responsibilities as well as their tenants. Lady Anne was determined to set such matters right, and part of her constant moving between castles was her wish to see and be seen. One typical journey took her from Appleby to Brough, where she stayed three nights, then through Kirby Stephen and Wharton Park to Pendragon castle, where she stayed six nights, then up through Ravenstonedale towards Sedbergh and into Yorkshire, to John Otway her lawyer's house at Ingmire for one night. From there, she went by Kirby Lonsdale, Cowan Bridge, Ingleton, and Clapham, to stay one night at the inn at Settle before taking the direct route over the moors via Malham Tarn to her house at Barden Tower. There she stayed for several months before moving to Skipton 'where I then began to lie in the chamber wherein I was born into the world'.

A year went by, during which daughter, Margaret, came to stay with her flock of surviving children, until it was time to return to Westmorland, which she did by an adventurous route. Starting at Kilnsey in Wharfedale—one night at the house of a Mr Cuthbert Wades—Lady Anne went through Kettlewell and up Buckden Rake on a very ancient road, over Stake Moss to stay one night at another private house belonging to her cousin, Thomas Metcalfe, at Nappa in Ribblesdale. Next was up and over by Cotterdale, in Wensleydale 'where I think never coach went before', over Hell Gill bridge, where Hell Gill beck flows into the infant river Eden, and so down to Mallerstang and Pendragon castle again.

These roads were nothing more than unmade farm tracks, rough and often impassable in bad weather, which did not deter the redoubtable Lady Anne and her equally redoubtable coachman. The coach itself, a heavy box on wheels with a curtain for a door, no glass in windows and very primitive springing, was pulled by four (also redoubtable) horses, and sometimes six on a good road. There would have been two or more outriders to survey the way, but no need to be concerned about footpads in the far upper dales. Lady Anne's was the only coach going that way and nobody was going to rob the greatest personage in the district.

Also living fairly rough just now was son-in-law Tufton, earl of Thanet, caught up in a legal dispute and committed to the Fleet prison. The origin was the alms-house for the poor known as Sackville College, founded by the 2nd earl of Dorset and completed by the 3rf earl, Lady Anne's first husband, with the intention of funding being supplied by the Sackville estates. When the 3rd earl died in 1624, leaving massing debts, funding became in short supply and the trustees of the college sued the family for money. As John Tufton was the late Dorset's son-in-law, he was held responsible but refused payment, was arrested for contempt of the court's order, and, after a month in the Fleet, paid up.

It was usual for the circuit judges to stay at Appleby castle while the assizes were held, and so, on the special occasion of a trial of traitors, two of the most eminent judges in the land were given the baron's chamber and the best room in Caesar's Tower in January 1664. On trial were two of the conspirators of the so-called Farnley Wood plot, whereby a small number of ex-parliamentarians from the Leeds area gathered to stage a feeble attempt at a rebellion, went home without doing anything, and expected to hear no more of it. Alas for them, their erstwhile leader had turned informer and twenty-six of them were arrested, mostly held in Clifford's Tower in York, and hanged, drawn, and quartered on a single morning. Three of the rest met the same fate at Appleby.

The rest of the year was the usual mix of happiness and sadness among Lady Anne's extensive family. John Tufton died, possibly from something he had picked up in the Fleet prison, and first grandson Nicholas Tufton married Lady Elizabeth Boyle, daughter of the 2nd earl of Cork. The newlyweds, now the new earl and countess of Thanet, came to stay with their grandmother—and, in Elizabeth's case, godmother—as did daughter and newly widowed Lady Margaret with three of her flock.

Another of Margaret's daughters, Lady Frances, married Henry Drax, whose father, Sir James, had made an enormous fortune from the two new trades of sugar planting and slavery, both in Barbados. In due course, Frances was in labour with her first child. The baby died before it could come forth, Lady Frances died soon after and Henry went back to his plantations.

Removals from one castle to another continued with their traditional frequency, although the aging Lady Anne had come to prefer her horse-litter, a kind of bed slung on poles carried by a horse front and back, to the carriage where her women servants journeyed. Every removal, from Brough to Appleby or Appleby to Pendragon, was a fairly grand affair, with menservants on horseback and often some local worthies and tenants accompanying. Various members of the family came to see the great lady, and the family itself ever produced more news of births and deaths. Lady Mary Walter, fifth daughter of Lady Anne's daughter Margaret, gave birth to a son, named William, who died after less than three weeks. That was in 1671; a year later, she had another child, a daughter, and in January 1674, she had her third child, a son, after which she herself was carried off by the smallpox.

There was a freak storm in the island of Guernsey, where Lord Christopher Hatton had been made governor as a reward for his loyalty to the royalist cause. Lightning struck the magazine at Castle Cornet, the garrison and headquarters, and in the explosion, Lady Anne's granddaughter, Cecily, wife of the governor, and his mother, were killed.

Not long after, both Cecily's daughters died—great-grandchildren of Lady Anne—plus a third of that generation, son, Edward, of Margaret's final child, Anne, who was buried at St Michael's church, St Albans, where also lay his distant ancestor, Thomas Lord Clifford, killed at the first battle of the Wars of the Roses.

Lady Anne seems to have kept all her faculties in these final years, but no matter how willing the spirit, the flesh was weakening and she stayed more and more in her chamber at Brougham castle, her favourite place, receiving guests there and not stirring forth while they dined with her folks in other rooms. Her diary entries often included memories of long ago: 'I remembered how this day was 59 years since I went with my first Lord, Richard Earl of Dorset before King James ... where the King earnestly desired me to subscribe to an award which he intended to make ... but by God's grace I began to deny it, it being the first time I was ever before that King'.

Family visits were a regular feature, and lots of them, with many possibilities from that very large group of the nation's nobility, mostly created by Lady Anne's daughter, Margaret, her twelve children born in the twenty-three years between 1631 and 1654 and only two of them dying young. Gradually, though, Lady Anne's eighty-six years took their toll.

> Ecclesiastes III i & ii: To every thing there is a season, and a time to every purpose under the heaven; A time to be born, and a time to die; a time to plant, and a time to pluck up that which is planted.

Samuel Grasty, the Brougham parson, came to Lady Anne's chamber to conduct her Sunday service, including sermon, and so her time came:

> March 1676. Upon the 18th day I did see Thomas Wright the Quaker in my chamber and saw him paid for 12 bushels of malt for a brewing

of beer for my House. I went not out of my chamber today. Upon the 19th day, being Palm Sunday, this morning I had a very violent fit of the wind, so that it caused me to fall into a swooning fit for about half an hour together, so as I thought I should have died, but it pleased God that I recovered and was better afterward. And today there dined with my folks in the Painted Room Master Grasty our parson, and my two farmers here, namely Wm Spedding and his wife and Jeffrey Blamire and his son, who after dinner came into my chamber and I kissed the woman and took the men by the hand. And a little after Master Grasty said Common Prayer and sung a Psalm as usual. I went not out of my chamber today.

Upon the 20th day I remembered how this day was 60 years since I and my blessed mother gave our answer that we would not stand to the judgement concerning my inheritance, which did spin out a great deal of trouble to us, yet God turned it for the best. I went not out of my chamber today.

Upon the 21st day, I went not out of my chamber today.

The diary entry for the 22nd day was completed by Lady Anne's steward:

At about 6 o'clock in the afternoon, after she had endured all her pains with a most Christian fortitude, always answering those that asked how she did with 'I thank God I am very well'—which were her last words directed to mortals, she, with much cheerfulness, in her own chamber at Brougham Castle, wherein her noble father was born and her blessed mother died, at the age of 86 years yielded up her precious soul into the hands of her merciful Redeemer.

Obituary

We shall have to imagine this. There were no obituaries in Lady Anne's day, and no newspapers in which to publish them. Had the *Cumberland and Westmorland Herald* been going then, doubtless the entire issue would have been filled with tributes, and only a tiny space allowed that week for the livestock prices from Penrith market.

The nearest thing to an obituary, apart from the eulogy at the funeral service, with what seemed like the whole of Westmoreland and Craven within and without the church, might be a sermon by the lord bishop of Carlisle, Bishop Rainbow, perhaps at the church of St Ninian at Brougham, rebuilt by Lady Anne after years of neglect of the original Norman fabric.

This bishop was famous for his sermons and for his many activities to help the poor; he was something of a Christian radical. Few of his words have survived and so we must imagine his address on the subject of Lady Anne Clifford, taking as his text: Matthew XVIII xxiv: 'It is easier for a camel to go through the eye of a needle, than for a rich man to enter the Kingdom of God'.

He would have spoken with vigour on the differences in Godly practices between rich and poor women:

> I have noticed that some gentlewomen with money and time to spare, will set aside a great part of each day to prayer and study of the Bible, and will meet with like minded souls for long and earnest debates on the progress of their own salvation. Those less fortunate, the poor women, who have to work through every hour that God sends, cannot offer Him

such an amount of devotion. So, we might conclude, that the Kingdom of Heaven is much peopled with gentlewomen, who have earned their passage by praising the Lord the most and by giving to the church the larger quantities of hassocks and gold altar cloths.

The poor women do have an advantage, according to Saint Matthew and Our Lord Jesus Christ. Mayhap these pious gentlewomen are trying to counterbalance the camellish quantity of their wealth and easeful life with sufficient quantity of piety. The poor women meanwhile must sweep the church rather than give it silver, and must carry God in their hearts at every turn rather than sit in a circle with their samplers, praying and praising God with every stitch. And for the men, well, men largely leave the practising of Godly things to the women. Attendance at church is thought by most men to be sufficient unto the Lord, without concerning Him over much with their philosophies.

Let me commend unto you, therefore, the life and works of our dear departed Lady Anne Clifford, a countess twice over and cousin to kings and queens, a woman who moved in the highest and richest circles and who, by the reckoning of the times we live in, outranked by far every one she was likely to meet. And yet, she forswore all of that glister and splendour of Court and left it to shepherd her flocks in the north, to see that all her folk were treated well, to build almshouses at Appleby, restore this church and do many good works. I doubt if her name will echo down the ages as would one who built a golden dome in London or kept warm the bed of King Charles. That is the way of this world but it is the way of the next world that my Lady Anne understood so well, and at our first Christmas without her, let us remember her. The Blessing of God Almighty, the Father, the Son, and the Holy Ghost, be upon you, and remain with you for ever. Amen.